No Uncertain Salvation

Contributors

Dr. J. D. Abbott, General Superintendent
The Wesleyan Church

J. A. Coffey, General Evangelist
The Wesleyan Church

Dr. William S. Deal, General Evangelist
The Wesleyan Church

Herbert Dongell, Professor of Religion
Central Wesleyan College

Dr. Robert H. Heckart, General Evangelist
The Wesleyan Church

Dr. Robert W. McIntyre, General Superintendent
The Wesleyan Church

Dr. Virgil A. Mitchell, General Superintendent
The Wesleyan Church

L. B. Reese, General Evangelist
The Wesleyan Church

Joe C. Sawyer, General Secretary of Extension and Evangelism
The Wesleyan Church

Dr. Harold K. Sheets, Former General Superintendent
The Wesleyan Church

Dr. Melvin H. Snyder, General Superintendent
The Wesleyan Church

Dr. W. L. Surbrook, General Superintendent Emeritus
The Wesleyan Church

No Uncertain Salvation

Edited by Keith W. Drury 83/ c.1

**The Wesley Press
Marion, Indiana**

First Wesleyan Church Library
1300 South Knox Court
Denver, Colorado 80219

234.5
W 513
no

International Standard Book Number: 0-89827-003-0

The Wesley Press; Marion, Indiana 46952

© 1979 by The Wesley Press. All rights reserved.

First edition published 1979

Printed in the United States of America

Contents

	Page
Preface	9
The Grounds of Our Faith, *Melvin H. Snyder*	11
Man's Worst and God's Best, *Robert W. McIntyre*	27
The Nature of Justification, *Virgil A. Mitchell*	41
The Nature of Sanctification, *J. D. Abbott*	55
Why I Believe in Holiness, *William S. Deal*	73
Paul's Plea for Purity, *Herbert Dongell*	79
The Central Idea of Christianity, *L. B. Reese*	83
That Missing Note of Victory, *Harold K. Sheets*	87
Experiential Sanctification, *W. L. Surbrook*	91
Endowment of Power, *J. A. Coffey*	95
The Basic Truth of Pentecost, *Robert H. Heckart*	99
Steps to the Spirit-filled Life, *Joe C. Sawyer*	103

Preface

This book, *No Uncertain Salvation,* presents messages and articles by persons of the Wesleyan-Arminian persuasion on subjects directly related to God's marvelous provision for man's redemption. It is done as with one mouth, with a voice like a trumpet.

At the dedication of Solomon's Temple the priests blew upon their trumpets at the time of sacrifice. On other occasions the sound of this instrument introduced ceremonies and sacrifices. In this book twelve of God's servants give expression to truths that are both biblical and basic to salvation. They do so with certain and definite clarity. The Apostle Paul observed that only a distinct and certain sound of the trumpet would rouse troops for battle. Today, from pulpit and classroom alike, God's Word must be declared in a sure, confident, and valid manner if hearers are to be brought to the Saviour and into the experience of Christian holiness.

The thrust of the book is toward holiness of heart and life with a view to emphasizing those biblical truths which convey that message. It is published by The Wesleyan Church as a part of its Holiness Evangelism Renewal Emphasis and with the prayer that its positive message shall provide valid and reliable guideposts for seekers of truth.

In a letter to his brother Charles in 1772, John Wesley wrote: "I find almost all our preachers, in every circuit, have done with Christian perfection. They say they believe it; but they never preach it; or not once in a quarter. What is to be done? Shall we let it drop, or make a point of it?" Mr. Wesley's decision is a matter of record.

Far from dropping the subject, the decision of The Wesleyan Church is to "make a point of it." This compilation of writings is meant to contribute to that end.

J. D. Abbott   Virgil A. Mitchell
Robert W. McIntyre   Melvin H. Snyder
General Superintendents

The Wesleyan Church

The Grounds of Our Faith

Melvin H. Snyder

Foundations are of utmost importance. This truth is graphically illustrated by our Lord in the parable of the two men, one wise and one foolish, who built their houses, one on the rock and the other on the sand. When the "floods came" and the "winds blew," the house built upon the rock stood because it was built upon a solid rock. But the house built upon the sand fell because it was no stronger than its foundation, "and great was the fall of it."[1]

It is only reasonable for rational men to ask, Is there a foundation for my faith that will stand the tests of time and eternity? Can a person have an unshakable conviction that there is one true and living God? Can a Christian really know that he has found "the way" and that he is right with God and with his fellowman? Wesleyans, along with a multitude of other evangelical Christians, believe that he can. They believe the one unshakable foundation is Jesus Christ our Lord. With Saint Paul they affirm, "For other foundation can no man lay that that is laid, which is Jesus Christ."

Upon what evidence do Wesleyans and other evangelicals accept this basis for their faith? Is it on the basis of some rational discovery, some philosophical theory, or some existential experience? No. The grounds of our faith is the Christian revelation. Ours is a revealed, not a discovered faith. For "faith cometh by hearing, and hearing by the word of God."[2]

Revelation is customarily divided into two major categories by theologians: 1) general revelation, and 2) special revelation — sometimes designated natural and supernatural or external and internal. "By general revelation we mean the disclosure of himself which God makes to all men in nature, in the constitution of the mind, and in the progress of human history."[3] The Holy Scriptures recognize general revelation. The psalmist affirmed, "The heavens declare the glory of God: and the firmament showeth his handiwork. Day unto day uttereth speech, and night unto night showeth knowledge. There is no speech nor language, where their voice is not heard. Their line is gone out through all the earth, and their words to the end of the world."[4] Paul, in describing the pagan world's unbelief, charged them with inexcusable ignorance: "Because that which may be known of God is manifest in them; for God hath showed it unto them. For the invisible things of him from the creation of the world are clearly seen, being understood by the things that are made, even his eternal power and Godhead; so that they are without excuse."[5] Paul is simply saying that the evidences of a Supreme Being are so clearly revealed in nature that unbelief is irrational, therefore inexcusable. The psalmist puts it even more bluntly, "The fool hath said in his heart, There is no God."[6] Had he used his head, he would not have come to such a foolish conclusion.

Much more could be said about general revelation but the limits of this discussion will not allow. I simply affirm that general revelation, as important as it is, is not sufficient to reveal God's redemptive action in behalf of man, His crowning creation. That required a special revelation.

"By special revelation we refer to the redemptive purpose of God manifested in Christ Jesus, as over against the more general revelation of his power and Godhead in the created universe, the constitution of man, and human history."[7] The documentary record of that revelation is the Bible. It "occupies an intermediate position between the partial revelation of God in nature and the perfect revelation of God in Christ — the Personal Word."[8] However, the Bible, the written Word, and Jesus Christ, the Living Word, are so inexorably united that to accept the validity and authority of one demands the acceptance of the validity and the authority of the other. Consistent with this view, Wesleyans take their stand with Jesus and the apostles who, without a single exception, accepted the absolute authority and inerrancy of the Word written. In fact, we only know the words and works of Jesus through the Word written, as recorded in the Old Testament prophetically and in the New Testament historically.

Wesleyans, personally and collectively, express their faith in this intermediate revelation in the following words: "The Holy Scriptures contain all things necessary to salvation; so that whatsoever is not read therein, nor may be proved thereby, is not to be required of any man, that it should be believed as an article of faith, or be thought requisite or necessary to salvation. We do understand the books of the Old and New Testaments to constitute the Holy Scriptures. These Scriptures we hold to be the inspired and infallibly written Word of God, fully inerrant in their original manuscripts and superior to all human authority."[9]

With such a high view of Scripture — the Word written — Wesleyans order their lives and minister in the name of Christ to the world. They are not unaware of the cynicism and unbelief on the part of many, both currently and in the past. Nor are they ignorant of the attacks of Satan upon this sure foundation through misguided and/or evil men who, having rejected general revelation, have no desire to know or ability to understand God's special revelation through Jesus Christ His Son as recorded in the Holy Scriptures — men who, like Satan, say, "Yea, hath God said . . .?"

Wesleyans are also aware of the current controversy within the evangelical movement over the use of the term "inerrant" in describing the infallibility of the Word written. Dr. Harold Lindsell's book, *The Battle for the Bible,* has not only brought this issue out into the open but has served a useful purpose in forcing the evangelical world to think and speak more definitively concerning its foundation, the Christ of the Bible. The Wesleyan Church unashamedly takes its stand with a host of evangelicals who believe the Scriptures to be "fully inerrant in their original manuscripts" in the classical understanding of the word "inerrant." In the words of Dr. Stephen Paine: "By the inerrancy of the Holy Scriptures is meant the complete dependability and trustworthiness of all the statements thereof, in terms of the significance intended by the writers. We do not distinguish it from infallibility. It is an article of faith having in view our Lord's attitude toward Scripture and that of the apostles, followed by the historic church."[10]

David Allen Hubbard, in stressing both the human and divine elements in Revelation, says, "At no time did God snatch the biblical authors from their settings; at no time did He transform them into other than what they were — citizens of an ancient time and place. Yet it is the wonder of His providence, the miracle of His power, that what they said and how they said it were precisely what He wanted."[11] This certainly is a statement supporting "full inerrancy" though it appears in the book, *Biblical Authority,* which basically supports "limited inerrancy." If, as Dr. Hubbard affirms, God by "the miracle of His power" caused them to say "precisely what He wanted," it is only consistent to believe that by the same "miracle of His power" He caused them to record "precisely what He wanted" since His whole purpose was to give man an objective written revelation of himself. This is the Bible's own claim; and if it is to be accepted as credible at all, this claim must also be accepted.[12]

It must be understood that this claim to full inerrancy and infallibility applies only to the autographs. The fact that these original manuscripts are not now extant in no way invalidates the principle involved — God spoke through selected men and caused His message and purpose to be recorded without error or mistake. If so, we have a sure guide to the Saviour and to heaven. If not, men would be left to their own subjective and existential evaluation of the Bible and its message and there would be no objective revelation that stands in judgment of man, but rather, man would stand in judgment of the revelation.

It was not until the 18th century and particularly the 19th and 20th centuries that the church itself began to question its own foundation. It is interesting to note John Wesley's reaction to this departure from belief in the plenary inspiration of the Scriptures. He says in a *Journal* entry of August 24, 1776, "I read Mr. Jenyns's admired tract on 'Internal Evidence of the Christian Religion.' He is undoubtedly a fine writer: but whether he is a Christian, Deist, or Atheist, I cannot tell. If he is a Christian, he betrays his own cause by averring, that 'all Scripture is not given by inspiration of God; but the writers of it were sometimes left to themselves, and consequently made some mistakes.' Nay, if there be any mistakes in the Bible, there may as well be a thousand. If there be one falsehood in that Book, it did not come from the God of truth."[13] Here Mr. Wesley's belief in full inspiration of the Scriptures is made crystal clear. He, of course, is speaking of the autographs for he believed in and practiced "textual criticism."

In the 19th century, T. DeWitt Talmage spoke eloquently for those of his generation who held to the full inspiration of the Scriptures despite the drift of a great number of preachers and churches. He observed: "A great London fog has come down upon some of the ministers and some of the churches in the shape of what is called 'advanced thought' in biblical interpretation. All of them, and without exception, deny the full inspiration of the Bible. Genesis is an allegory, and there are many myths in the Bible, and they philosophize and guess and reason and evolute until they land in a great continent of mud, from which I fear, for all eternity they will not be able to extricate themselves.

"The Bible is not only divinely inspired, but it is divinely protected in its present shape. You could have as easily, without detection, taken from the writings of Shakespeare, 'Hamlet,' and instituted in the place thereof Alexander Smith's drama as at any time during the last 1,500 years a man could have made any important change in the Bible without immediate detection."[14] Note that the great 19th-century pulpiteer expresses his complete confidence in the full inspiration of the original manuscripts and a protecting providence over the copies or translations. Most of us would agree that only the autographs were *actually* inspired and that accurate copies or translations may be said to be *virtually* inspired, inasmuch as they correctly reproduce the original.

As Geisler and Nix point out in their book, *A General Introduction to the Bible,* "Some have objected to what they consider a retreat to 'inerrant autographs' from errant copies, as if the doctrine of inspiration were created to protect the errancy of the Bible, as they chide that no one in modern times has ever seen these 'infallible originals.' While it may be true that no one in modern times has ever seen an infallible original, it is also true that no one has ever seen a fallible one either. In the light of this situation, it is well to note that the pursuit of the original renderings is at least an *objective science* (textual criticism) rather than a *subjective guess.*"

Upon what evidences then do Wesleyans accept the

final authority and full inerrancy of the Bible? The question is fair and should be answered intelligently and in meekness. Peter, the fisherman, not only became a fisher of men, but also a Christian apologist and exhorted his fellow believers "to be ready always to give an answer to every man that asketh you a reason of the hope that is in you, with meekness and fear."[15]

God has made man a rational being and never asks anything of him that is repugnant to sound reason. It is God who invites, "Come now and let us reason together."[16] Biblical faith is not credulity but is based upon indubitable evidence. Let us therefore call up the most credible witnesses:

First, the witness of the Bible itself. There are those who take exception to allowing the Bible to testify concerning itself, since its reliability and authority are the matter of investigation. Nonetheless, as Philip E. Hughes points out, "It is a common place of legal justice that any person standing trial has the right to engage in self-testimony. By itself, that is in the absence of the independent witness or other persons or circumstances, that self-testimony may or may not be true. The point is that it *may be true*, and so it must not be stifled. In the case of the Bible, it bears witness to itself in terms which, if true, are of the most vital consequences for the whole of mankind. Its witness must, therefore, be heard."[17]

Turning to the Old Testament, we find the prophets averring that they did not speak for, or of, themselves. Someone has counted and reported that the expression, "Thus saith the Lord . . ." and "The word of the Lord came unto me saying . . ." or similar affirmations occur 3,808 times in the Old Testament alone. Unless it be conceded that these were wicked men who, by some strange collusion over a period of many centuries, connived to deceive the human race, it must be admitted that they spoke and recorded the word of God. That they were not in illusion concerning God's voice is proved again and again by fulfilled prophecy.

Coming to the New Testament, we have corroborating witness by Jesus and the apostles that the Old Testament writers wrote the authoritative word of God. Jesus often appealed to the Old Testament scriptures as final authority and went so far as to say, "Till heaven and earth pass, one jot or one tittle shall in no wise pass from the law, till all be fulfilled."[18] An outstanding example of Christ's confidence in and reliance upon the Holy Scriptures is recorded by Luke in the discourse that transpired between Jesus and the disciples on the Emmaus Road following His resurrection. Seeking to restore their shattered faith, He jarred them into attention by saying, "O fools, and slow of heart to believe all that the prophets have spoken: Ought not Christ to have suffered these things, and to enter into his glory? And beginning at Moses and all the prophets, he expounded unto them in all the scriptures the things concerning himself."[19] Strange words indeed, if Moses and the prophets spoke only as fallible men. As always, the infallible Holy Spirit bore witness to His infallible word; for we read, "And they said one to another, Did not our heart burn within us, while he talked with us by the way and while he opened to us the Scriptures?"[20] Another outstanding example of Christ's full confidence in and reliance on the Old Testament scriptures is on the occasion of His mortal conflict with Satan in the wilderness. Three times He countered the tempter by saying, "It is written."[21] As the Son of Man, He skillfully wielded the sword of the Spirit which is the Word of God. It proved to be the end of controversy with Satan himself. Foolish men may doubt that God has spoken through the written Word, but not Satan, for we read, "The devils also believe, and tremble."[22]

Like their Master, the apostles often appealed to the authority of the Scriptures. Their faith in the unfolding revelation of God to them as apostles was predicted upon the authority and inerrancy of the Old Testament. Peter averred, "We have also a more sure word of prophecy; whereunto ye do well that ye take heed, as unto a light that shineth in a dark place, until the day dawn, and the day star arise in your hearts: Knowing this first, that no prophecy of the scripture is of any private interpretation. For the prophecy came not in old time by the will of man: but holy men of God spake as they were moved by the Holy Ghost."[23]

The New Testament, likewise, is not without its own self-testimony. If the Old Testament bears witness primarily to the One who is to come, the New Testament bears witness to the One who has come. It bears witness to Him who, in His person and actions as well as in His teachings, is the Word of God incarnate. We have here the record of the imperishable truth which Christ brought and taught. He did not hesitate to proclaim that heaven and earth would pass away, but that His words would not pass away.[24] He made the unqualified promise to His apostles that the Holy Spirit would teach them all things and bring to their remembrance all that He had spoken to them, and would lead them into all truth, revealing to them things that were to come.[25] As Philip E. Hughes so discerningly observes, "This is the very keystone of the New Testament and of the claims which it makes for itself."[26] In consistency with this promise, we find John affirming that the witness of his gospel is true[27] and Peter classifying Paul's epistles along with "the other scriptures."[28]

The second witness we would call to the stand is the witness of history. The presence of the church in this world is the outstanding witness of history to the Bible. Until modern times, the Bible was always acknowledged by the church to be the inspired Word of God. Though the early fathers were not always agreed on every doctrinal issue, they were united in their commitment to the Bible as the inspired Word of God. Never did they claim for their own writings the authority and inspiration they attributed to the Scripture. Most of the Reformers took the same position regarding the Scriptures. The traditions of the church were judged by the Scriptures, not vice versa.

There is evidence that the canon of Holy Scripture, particularly that of the New Testament (since that of the Old Testament had already been established), was not the result of arbitrary selection by the church councils, as some claim, but rather the recognition of an authority vested in the manuscripts themselves as they had been circulated among the churches. The claims made by the writers, just as was the case of the Old Testament, and witnessed to by the Holy Spirit was the deciding factor. As Philip E. Hughes points out, "If there were one external factor which played a decisive role in the fixing of the New Testament canon, it was the equating of canonicity with apostolicity. Books which were not of apostolic origin were not admissible as canonical."[29] Their divine authority derived from Christ, their divine Master, shines through the canonical books and brings to a conclusion a divine revelation which stands unshaken and unshakable. John, through that same divine authority, pronounces a curse upon all who add to or subtract from the words of his prophecy.[30] While this warning applies directly and primarily to the prophetic word in the Revelation, there is obviously an application to the entire revelation of Jesus Christ as given us in the canonical books. What we have begun in Genesis we have culminated in Revelation and sealed as God's authoritative word to the race.

Again, history attests the divine inspiration of the Bible by the radical transformation which the reception of its message has produced in the lives of men and women who have held the Bible to be more precious than any other possession and have been willing to suffer persecution, torture, and even death, rather than deny the truth by which they had been set free. Wesley's testimony is most pertinent at this point: "To candid, reasonable men, I am not afraid to lay open what have been the inmost thoughts of my heart. I have thought, 'I am a creature of a day, passing through life as an arrow through the air. I am a spirit come from God, and returning to God: Just hovering over the great gulf; till, a few moments hence, I am no more seen; I drop into an unchangeable eternity!' I want to know one thing — the way to heaven; how to land safe on that happy shore. God himself has condescended to teach the way: For this very end he came from heaven. He hath written it down in a Book. O, give me that Book! At any price, give me the Book of God! I have it: Here is knowledge enough for me. Let me be *homo unius libri.*"[31] The dynamic influence of John Wesley's ministry upon 18th-century England and the reforms which followed cannot be explained apart from his unshakable faith in the absolute authority of the Bible.

The history of our own day gives another attestation to the power and authority of the Word written. At the very time the liberal higher critics had written off mass evangelism and discarded an authoritative Bible, God raised up Billy Graham to demonstrate the power of His Word. Hear his own testimony:

> "In 1949 I had been having a great many doubts concerning the Bible. I thought I saw apparent contradictions in scripture. Some things I could not reconcile with my restricted concept of God. When I stood up to preach, the authoritative note so characteristic of all great preachers of the past was lacking. Like hundreds of other young seminary students, I was waging the intellectual battle of my life. The outcome could certainly affect my future ministry.
>
> "In August of that year I had been invited to Forest Home, a Presbyterian Conference Center high in the mountains outside of Los Angeles. I remember walking down a trail tramping into the woods, and almost wrestling with God. I dueled with my doubts, and my soul seemed to be caught in a cross fire. Finally, in desperation, I surrendered my will to the Living God revealed in the Scripture. I knelt before the open Bible and said, 'Lord, many things in this Book I do not understand. But Thou hast said, "The just

shall live by faith." All I have received from Thee, I have taken by faith. Here and now, by faith, I accept the Bible as Thy Word. I take it all. I take it without reservations. Where there are things I cannot understand, I will reserve judgment until I receive more light. If this pleases Thee, give me authority as I proclaim Thy Word, and through that authority convict men of sin and turn sinners to the Saviour.'

"Within six weeks we started our Los Angeles Crusade, which is now history. During that Crusade I discovered the secret that changed my ministry. I stopped trying to prove that the Bible was true. I had settled in my own mind that it was, and this faith was conveyed to the audience. Over and over again I found myself saying, 'The Bible says . . .' I felt as though I were merely a voice through which the Holy Spirit was speaking.

"Authority created faith. Faith generated response, and hundreds of people were impelled to come to Christ. A Crusade scheduled for three weeks lengthened into eight weeks with hundreds of thousands of people in attendance. The people were not coming to hear great oratory, nor were they interested merely in my ideas. I found they were desperately hungry to hear what God had to say through His Holy Word. I felt as though I had a rapier in my hand and, through the power of the Bible, was slashing deeply into men's consciences, leading them to surrender to God. Does not the Bible say of itself, 'For the word of God is quick, and powerful, and sharper than any two-edged sword, piercing even to the dividing asunder of soul and spirit, and of the joints and marrow, and is a discerner of the thoughts and intents of the heart' (Hebrews 4:12)?

"I found that the Bible became a flame in my hands. That flame melted away unbelief in the hearts of the people and moved them to decide for Christ. The Word became a hammer breaking up stony hearts and shaping them into the likeness of God. Did not God say, 'I will make my words in thy mouth fire' (Jeremiah 5:14) and 'Is not my word like as a fire? . . . and like a hammer that breaketh the rock in pieces?' (Jeremiah 23:29)."[32]

Third, the witness of God, the Holy Spirit. Mr. Graham's experience also testifies to the fact that God, by His Spirit, witnesses to the truth of the Bible. Having committed himself to its truthfulness, he proclaimed it in faith and found that it would do exactly what it claimed. Men's consciences were pricked, sin confessed, and faith activated — all through the power of the Word. He found that the witness of God is greater than the witness of man and needs no support, but stands firm by itself. The Holy Spirit himself witnesses to the truthfulness of the record which He authored through human agents whom He had prepared for this holy task. Only through His ministry is the Word authenticated to the heart and mind of every true believer. It is only through the ministry of the Holy Spirit that men are brought to faith in Christ as Saviour, and *that* faith is predicated upon the Word written as we find it recorded in God's special revelation which we call the Bible. Dr. Hughes has aptly said, "As the witness of the Holy Spirit, this testimony is objective; as an internal witness within the believer, it is subjective. As at the same time both objective and subjective, this witness is completely impregnable. He who experiences it cannot gainsay it. He who gainsays it has not experienced it, and should search his heart as to why this is so." He goes on to make a plea to those who have missed the way to put the Scriptures to the test: "In all charity and humility we would invite those to whom this internal witness of God, the Holy Spirit, is something strange to consider whether they are not lacking one of the essentials of genuine Christianity and whether, consequently, they are in any proper position to assail the doctrine of the inspiration of the Bible. We would urge them to pray that God would grant them the witness of the Holy Spirit, to convince and enlighten both heart and intellect."[33]

Wesleyans should remember always that the primary purpose and function of the Scripture is to lead us to Christ. Paul admonished Timothy that the Holy Scriptures were able to make him "wise unto salvation through faith which is in Jesus Christ."[34] John, the human agent used by the Holy Spirit to give us the gospel which bears his name, his general epistle, as well as two personal epistles, and the Revelation, declares: "These are written, that ye might believe that Jesus is the Christ, the Son of God; and that believing ye might have life through his name."[35] Here Wesleyans take their stand upon the sure foundation of

Jesus Christ as revealed in the Old and New Testaments and witnessed to their hearts by the Holy Spirit. The grounds of their faith could hardly be stated more properly than by Mr. Whitehead when he averred, "The Bible contains the mind of God, the state of man, the way of salvation, the doom of sinners, the happiness of believers. Its doctrines are holy, its precepts are binding, its decisions are immutable. Read it to believe, believe it to be safe, practice it to be holy. It contains light to direct you, food to support you, and comfort to cheer you. It is the traveler's guide, the pilgrim's staff, the pilot's compass, the soldier's sword, and the Christian's charter. Here Paradise is restored, Heaven opened and the gates of Hell disclosed. Christ is its grand subject, our good its design, and the glory of God its end. It should fill the memory, rule the heart, and guide the feet. Read it slowly, daily, prayerfully. It is a mine of wealth, a paradise of glory, and a river of pleasure. It is given you in life, will be opened at the Judgment, and will be remembered forever. It involves the highest responsibility, will reward the greatest labor, and condemn all who trifle with its contents."[36]

With this faith in God's Holy Word, Wesleyans accept and proclaim all of the cardinal doctrines of the Bible. We believe that central to these doctrines is God's call to holiness of heart and life. Therefore, we proclaim this scriptural doctrine of holiness and exhort all fellow believers to make a complete consecration of all their ransomed powers and to claim by faith this rich provision of God's grace.

Notes

1. Matthew 7:24-27.
2. Romans 10:17.
3. H. Orton Wiley, *Introduction to Christian Theology*, (Kansas City, Missouri: Beacon Hill Press, 1969), p. 37.
4. Psalm 19:1-4.
5. Romans 1:19-20.
6. Psalm 14:1.

7. Wiley, *op. cit.*, p. 40.
8. Ibid, p. 41.
9. *The Discipline of The Wesleyan Church*, (Marion, Indiana: The Wesleyan Publishing House, 1976). Articles of Religion, Section V., The Sufficiency and Full Authority of the Holy Scriptures for Salvation.
10. Stephen Paine, *The Bible: What is meant by calling it inerrant?; The Wesleyan Advocate*, Vol. 130, No. 162; May 1, 1972, p. 8.
11. David Allen Hubbard, *Biblical Authority*, Jack Rogers, editor; (Waco, Texas: Word, 1978) Chapter Title: "The Current Tension: Is there a Way Out?"
12. Exodus 34:1, Deuteronomy 10:2; Exodus 34:27; Jeremiah 32; John 20:31.
13. John Wesley, *Journal*, Vol. IV., (London: Wesleyan Conference Office, 1867) p. 77.
14. T. DeWitt Talmage.
15. I Peter 3:15.
16. Isaiah 1:18.
17. Philip E. Hughes, *Basic Christian Doctrine*, Carl F. H. Henry, editor, (New York: Holt, Rinehart and Winston, 1962) p. 15.
18. Matthew 5:18.
19. Luke 24:25-27.
20. Luke 24:32.
21. Matthew 4:4,7,10.
22. James 2:19.
23. II Peter 1:19-21.
24. Matthew 24:35.
25. John 14:26; 16:13.
26. Hughes, *op. cit.*, p. 17.
27. John 21:24.
28. II Peter 3:15-16.
29. Hughes, *op. cit.*, p. 17.
30. Revelation 22:18-19.
31. *The Works of John Wesley*, Volume V (Grand Rapids, Michigan: Zondervan) Preface, pp. 2-3.
32. Billy Graham, *"Biblical Authority in Evangelism"; Christianity Today*, Vol. 1, No. 1, October 15, 1956, p. 5 ff, © 1956. Used by permission.
33. Hughes, *op. cit.*, p. 19.
34. II Timothy 3:15.
35. John 20:31.
36. Wiley, *op. cit.*, p. 37.

Man's Worst and God's Best

Robert W. McIntyre

Two of the most significant acts in God's unfolding drama of sin and salvation are played in a garden. In a garden man did his worst when he rebelled against God and opened the door to the depravity of the human race. In a garden God did His best when He gave His Son to die for men's sins and then made Him victor over the grave. One unleashed depravity upon the earth; the other opened the door to deliverance.

The lasting fruitage of the Fall of Man, Original or Birth Sin, is described in Article of Religion VIII in *The Wesleyan Discipline* as follows: "Original sin standeth not in the following of Adam (as the Pelagians do vainly talk), but it is the corruption of the nature of every man, that naturally is engendered of the offspring of Adam, whereby man is very far gone from original righteousness, and of his own nature inclined to evil, and that continually."[1]

God's antidote for this poison is described in Article of Religion IX. The Atonement: "The offering of Christ, once made, through His sufferings and meritorious death on the cross, is that perfect redemption and propitiation for the sins of the whole world, both original and actual. There is none other ground of salvation from sin but that alone. The atonement is sufficient for every individual of Adam's race, and is graciously efficacious to the salvation of the irresponsible from birth, or to the righteous who have become irresponsible, and to the children in innocency, but is efficacious to those who reach the age of responsibility only when they repent and believe."[2]

In any theological system the doctrine of sin and the doctrine of the atonement must stand together. Our belief as to what Christ accomplished on the cross must be in harmony with what we believe to be man's need as a result of the Fall. The cross is the solution: the problem is sin. Had there been no sin, atonement would have been no more necessary than it was necessary for Christ to atone for himself. We cannot effectively minister to people's many hurts until we treat the root of those hurts, which is sin.

Commenting on the admission of a widely known psychologist that Freudian theory had failed, and his confession that "I see no alternative but to turn again to the old, painful but also promising possibility that man is preeminently a social creature, or, in a theological phrase, a child of God," Merne A. Harris and Richard S. Taylor observe: "Here is a frank admission that guilt, the cause of most mental illness, is a moral problem, and its solution is theological. Unfortunately, the clergymen who, in their feverish anxiety to be up to date, have discarded their doctrines of sin and salvation are no better off than the frustrated psychiatrist."[3]

Sin cost Jesus' death, sin merits the wrath of God, sin discounts Calvary. A gospel of good news must start with basic need, and that need is the solution to each person's own sin problem.

John Fletcher said that in every religion there is a principal truth or error, which, like the first link of a chain, necessarily draws after it all the parts with which it is essentially connected. In the Christian religion this first link is the fact of sin.[4]

This issue has always been critical, but it is particularly critical today. Antinomianism, less politely called lawlessness, is attempting a subtle invasion of the minds of evangelicals, including Wesleyans. Certain popular speakers and publications are among its tools. Its tendency is to blur the sin issue; to introduce Christ as Saviour, but not keeper; to present Him as a helper, rather than Lord; and to react to the legalism of other days by almost ignoring completely His distinctive ethical demands upon those who profess a personal relationship to Him.

When sin is not seen as exceeding sinful and inherited depravity is seen at the best as common humanity and at the worst as a slight inconvenience, it is little wonder if the holiness message suffers neglect. What is there left to be delivered from?

To present a wrong view of sin is to lead astray those who look to you for guidance; to present a right view is to set a straight course down the road of Christian experience.

For the source of the inherited tendency to sinfulness (or instinct, as one calls it), we turn, of course, back to the Garden. There the primal pair, still enjoying the holiness in which they were created, came under the influence of Satan. Persuaded but uncoerced, in an act which had moral quality because it was freely done, they chose to disobey specific instructions which had been clearly communicated to them.[5] Eve made the first response and then led her husband in a similar act; but his was the critical one, since he, as the original creation, represented the whole race yet unborn.[6] John Wesley calls him in this capacity "a public person" and "the representative man."

J. Kenneth Grider believes that Arminius was right in saying that there are two kinds of law, natural and symbolical, and that Adam in the Garden broke the latter kind. A natural law, says Arminius, is "imprinted on the mind of man," so that man can see it to be needful; e.g., that he is to love God and other persons. A symbolical one is the kind which man cannot see to be significant by use of rational and moral capacities. Arminius defines it as "one that prescribes or forbids an act which, in itself, is neither agreeable nor disagreeable to God . . . which serves for the purpose that God may try whether man is willing to yield obedience to him, solely . . . because it has been the pleasure of God to require such obedience."[7]

There has never been another sin quite like that first one in the Garden. The commandment that was broken related strictly to the Garden of Eden. We have no record of that particular law being given any time before or since. The sin of Adam which had its effect upon the whole race cannot be repeated. It stands as an example of the far-reaching influence of sin. It is the "one" sin of which Paul speaks in Romans 5:12, 15-19.

Its effect upon man has been described in various ways. Grider sums it up:

> You see him cowering behind a bush, afraid to be confronted by the Lord God, who seeks out sinners. A little later you see him coming out of hiding and, in shameless impudence, proposing to climb up into heaven by a tower of his own building. Much later, with sin's progressive worsening, you see him rushing out upon the God-man when it was night and shuttling Him off to be crucified in short order.
>
> And that is not all, by any means. In the succeeding centuries he has not been only "a lost waif in a lost world"[8] but, in his fallenness, a rabid dog infecting whatever he touches. An angel has had him by the hand, but Satan has had him by the heart.[9] He has grasped what is worthless and left untouched things that are priceless. And the more he has reached for what he has liked, the less he has liked what he has reached for.[10]

Sin is the exact opposite of holiness. It is not what man was made for. It does not fulfill God's design for him. It cannot accomplish God's end for him. In his *Studies in Biblical Holiness,* Donald S. Metz says:

> The ultimate spiritual antithesis is the opposition between holiness and sin. Man was designed for holiness, created in holiness and destined for holiness. But sin marred the original design, ruined the state of innocent holiness,

and now threatens man's destiny. . . .

Such is the tragic situation of man. With Godlike qualities and unlimited potential, he finds himself living far below his possibilities. With holiness as his original destiny, man finds himself groveling in the slime of depraved living. The great human tragedy is the reality of sin. The grand human hope is the possibility of holiness. Holiness and sin represent the basic and permanent clash of opposites. Holiness represents the essential nature of God. Sin stands for the denial of holiness and opposition to God's very existence. . . .

It is possible to understand the nature of holiness only to the extent that we understand the nature of sin. Among the great focal themes of the biblical revelation — God, man, sin, and redemption — sin is seen as the ugly intruder.[11]

Many questions are raised by a discussion of the origin of sin. One of these is: How can a holy being sin? In this brief space let us only say that man was made in God's moral image. He was holy, but not absolutely so, as God is. He was a free moral agent. Freedom of choice demands occasions by which character may be tested. By definition, temptation includes the possibility of response. The opportunity for sin presented it as attractive and beneficial. But it was also clearly presented as a challenge to what God had said. Eve, who did not have as much at stake, yielded first. Adam then had the additional pressure of his wife's solicitation and the knowledge that she had already broken God's law. Since then, other good men have yielded under considerably less pressure than that.

The Article of Religion on Original Sin in *The Wesleyan Discipline* still carries the historic opening format: "Original sin standeth not in the following of Adam (as the Pelagians do vainly talk)," referring to an early controversy probably long since forgotten, except by theologians. Since the statement is there, permit this summary of the teachings of Pelagianism: all sin originates in the abuse of freedom. Man is born without any bias to evil, and therefore character is due wholly to the nature of his choices. The seven points of Pelagianism were:

> 1. Adam was created mortal and would have died, even if he had not sinned.
>
> 2. Adam's sin injured, not the human race, but only himself.
>
> 3. Newborn infants are in the same condition as Adam before the Fall.
>
> 4. The whole human race neither dies because of Adam's sin nor rises on account of Christ's resurrection.
>
> 5. Infants, even though not baptized, attain eternal life.
>
> 6. The law is as good a means of salvation as the gospel.
>
> 7. Even before Christ some men lived who did not commit sin.[12]

When Wesleyan theology is not understood, Calvinists sometimes accuse Wesleyans of being Pelagian.

One other question which must be treated is that of the transmission of original sin or inherited depravity.

Let it first be acknowledged that sin is almost universally recognized as both an act and a state.

For sin as an act, definitions of varying lengths and depth may be found. Definitions by Wesleyan-Arminian authors sum up to: sin is rebellion, which implies both knowledge and willfulness.[13] The moral quality of the act lies in the intention rather than in the act itself. A believer whose heart is open and tender may have confidence. It is the responsibility of the Spirit to lead us into all truth. Condemnation will be specific enough to be confessed and forgiven.

The sin Adam committed was his own, but it had racial consequences because of his position as the first man. In Romans 5:12 the King James rendering is "all have sinned," but the tense of the Greek makes it read "all sinned." When Adam sinned, we were all there — not in a real way, as Augustine taught, but we sinned because our representative did and suffered loss even as an entire school might if its representative loses at a track meet. This is why Adam is racially significant, according to Paul, and why Adam is contrasted with Christ in Romans 5:12-21 and I Corinthians 15:21-22, 45-52.[14]

Wesleyanism believes that men in an unrelieved state of total depravity cannot cooperate with God, but that whatever guilt accrued from "being there" when Adam sinned was removed by justification through Christ — that is, that in whatever way we "all sinned" in Adam we were "all justified" in Christ, and that, through the Spirit, man is now given the ability to cooperate or respond to the appeal of the gospel. Man is responsible for his own acts of sin. He is not responsible for having inherited depravity, but he is responsible if he keeps it after a way of deliverance has been opened to him.

The authors of *God, Man & Salvation* draw a picture of inherited depravity slightly different from that usually seen:

> Depravity, original sin, inbred sin, or carnality — by whatever name the fact may be described — is best defined not as a thing, an entity or quantity having ontic status, but as the moral condition of a personal being. It is caused by estrangement, severance, alienation, "deprivity," or loss. It is manifested in attitudes, dispositions, tendencies, or propensities — in psychological terminology, a state of readiness or conditioning. Speaking, like Paul, after the manner of men (Romans 6:19; I Corinthians 15:32; Galatians 3:15), one may say that original sin is more like disease, poverty, blindness, darkness, or the corruption of a severed branch than it is like a root, a cancer, or a decayed tooth.[15]

Paul speaks of this interior sin as a law.[16] It is a law from the standpoint of its uniformity of operation. It is consistent, in that it always impels toward godlessness or evil. Unlike some other laws, the individual had no part in enacting it — it was there when we came. Since we did not pass it, we cannot repeal it. Its effect can be resisted, but only God can deliver from its influence.

Inbred sin, then, is of somewhat the same nature as Adam's primitive holiness. It is a tendency to evil as his was a tendency to good. It is not absolute in the sense of being irrevocable. As long as man is a moral being he has freedom to choose. It is God's grace that quickens those who are dead in trespasses and sins.[17] Each of us personally decides whether we will harbor the sin tendency or submit to God's overtures of grace and walk in the Spirit.

In sin man is seen at his worst, and in some sense the worst of all these was that apparently simple act of picking forbidden fruit in a garden. The scope of that one act can only be comprehended by reflecting on the chaos of the years that have followed.

But the depravity of the human heart with all of its consequences is not the end of the story. Over against man's worst, God set His very best. Although our message must begin with sin, it doesn't end there. Immediately after the Fall, God began to unfold an amazing plan. In the words of Article IX, "The offering of Christ, once made, . . . is . . . perfect redemption."[18] Simply stated, that is it.

In our community a particularly savage crime was committed one night in early fall of 1978. An aged woman living alone was brutally molested, beaten, and killed in an upstairs bedroom. Police investigating the crime followed a trail of blood to a local "topless" bar. When they caught the young man who had committed the crime, they learned that he had suffered nosebleed in the bar and had gone from there to the house where the woman was attacked. But the trail of blood was clear.

There is a trail of blood in the Bible that begins in Genesis with the death of the animals God slew to clothe Adam and Eve — and probably to show them how to make sacrifice for sin. It continues through Abel's offering and the Passover scene on down through the bloody rituals of the Tabernacle in the wilderness. It appears again and again on the pages of the Old Testament, leaps the chasm into the New, and leads on up to the brow of a hill called Calvary. From there it leads across page after page until we come to the Revelation where we hear a voice crying, "For the accuser of our brethren is cast down . . . and they overcame him by the blood of the Lamb, and by the word of their testimony."[19]

Probably no one said it better than Jesus himself, at the Last Supper: "This is my blood of the new testament which is shed for many for the remission of sins."[20]

To begin at the beginning, any consideration of the atonement must turn first to God. It is He who was sinned against. His law was violated. His kindness was ignored. His love was spurned. But the constancy of His love opened the door for restoration. The plan was His, although it cost Him His Son, and, in some sense, himself. The Incarnation was born in the mind of God before Christ was born in a crowded stable. The sacrificial death, too, issued from God's love.[21] It was His wrath which was activated against sin. Wrath is a word we have difficulty understanding when it describes the attitude of a holy, loving God, but it is the most appropriate one to describe the response of a sensitive, holy God to the ungodliness and wickedness of men.[22] It is this wrath which will finally be poured out on the unrepentant. Yet in the face of wrath love devised a plan. Finally, in the cross, both love and wrath are seen — love for a world, and wrath against sin.[23]

Atonement was a necessity — because the gulf between a majestic, holy God and sinful, rebellious creatures was unbridged. Sin had separated man from God.[24] Sin had robbed man of a loving Father and had robbed God of the fellowship of His creatures. His holiness kept them from approaching Him, while His love drew Him to them. Some link, or common ground, was necessary if fellowship were to be restored. God himself provided the offering and His Son volunteered to carry out the plan.

With its origin in God, the atonement satisfied His own holiness and opened an avenue by which His creatures could approach Him.

Atonement is seen also as a necessity from a governmental standpoint. God has established a moral law, which man has broken. The breaking of law carries with it a penalty. The Righteous Judge cannot ignore the broken law or the lawbreaker. The penalty must be meted out. In suffering the penalty, Christ satisfies justice and opens the way for the lawbreaker to be forgiven.

The atonement is seen also as a necessity from the standpoint of ultimate love. The cross is both the climax of man's rebellion and the ultimate demonstration of God's love. One who views the cross in rebellion suffers eternal loss; to view it in love and accept its merits is to become a new creature and to enter the way of love.

The term, "the blood of Christ," appears more than thirty times on the pages of the New Testament. It is thought by some to be the equivalent of "life." Others view it as signifying "death." Still others believe that it is but another way of saying "the cross of Christ," or "the crucifixion." The blood is significant, not as a material substance, but because of what it represents — the provision of salvation through the death of the Son of God on the cross.[25]

Such a price can scarcely be comprehended.

Robert Coleman tells in *Written in Blood* of a little boy who was told by his doctor that he could save his sister's life by giving her some blood. The six-year-old girl was near death — a victim of a disease from which the boy had made a marvelous recovery two years earlier. Her only chance for restoration was a blood transfusion from someone who had previously conquered the illness. Since the two children had the same rare blood type, the boy was the ideal donor.

"Johnny, would you like to give your blood for Mary?" the doctor asked.

The boy hesitated. His lower lip started to tremble. Then he smiled and said, "Sure, Doc, I'll give my blood for my sister."

Soon the two children were wheeled into the operating room — Mary, pale and thin; Johnny, robust and the picture of health. Neither spoke, but when their eyes met, Johnny grinned.

As his blood siphoned into Mary's veins, one could almost see new life come into her tired body. The ordeal was almost over when Johnny's brave little voice broke the silence. "Say, Doc, when do I die?"

It was only then that the doctor realized what the moment of hesitation, that trembling of the lip, meant. Johnny actually thought that in giving his blood to his sister he was giving up his life. And in that brief moment he had made his great decision![26]

Such was the decision made in the councils of heaven in fulfilling atonement's plan.

Dr. W. A. Criswell sees Barabbas as typical of one for whom another has died:

> Of all the people who ever lived, there was no one who had the idea of the atonement of Christ, of his substitutionary death, as did Barabbas. Barabbas was a robber, an insurrectionist, a murderer. He was imprisoned to be executed by crucifixion, according to the Roman practice. One day at nine o'clock in the morning, on a Friday, a Roman legionnaire swung open the iron gates of the prison and called, "Barabbas." The murderer and insurrectionist came to the door expecting to be crucified. Instead, the Roman legionnaire said, "Barabbas, you are free."
>
> Amazed, the insurrectionist walked out to freedom. Just beyond he saw the form of a humble, meek, and lowly man staggering beneath the weight of a heavy cross. When the cross was lifted high, with two of Barabbas' companions nailed to crosses on either side, one can see Barabbas as he elbowed his way through the throng and stood there looking at Jesus, who was nailed on the center cross. He might have said, "That man has taken my place." No one could ever have as poignant an understanding of the meaning of atonement as Barabbas.[27]

"Sufficient for every individual," our Article of Religion says.[28] No one is left out. In some sense we were all there that day, as we were all in that other garden so long ago.

Dr. Robert G. Lee tells of an unforgettable experience he had the first time he visited Calvary on a tour of Israel. His excitement was such that he soon outdistanced his guide in climbing the hill. As he reached the summit and stood there at the very place where his Lord poured out His blood, the great preacher's emotions were so stirred that his body started to tremble. When at last the breathless guide caught up to him, he asked, "Sir, have you been here before?" For a moment, there was a throbbing silence. Then in a whispered tone Dr. Lee replied, "Yes, I was here nearly two thousand years ago."[29]

The death of Jesus Christ on Calvary was an adequate answer for the deepest need of every person. "Divine love saw the alienation of sin and found a way of reconciliation. Divine love saw the guilt of sin and found a way of pardon. Divine love saw the depravity of sin and found a way of restoration. Divine love saw the condemnation of sin and found a method of justification. Divine love saw the defilement of sin and found a way of cleansing. Divine love saw the death of sin and found a way of eternal life. Divine love saw and sought and found."[30]

Donald Metz refers to "the pessimistic doctrine of innate depravity and the optimistic doctrine of Christian perfection."[31] Thank God for the difference! Thank God for sin's antidote! Thank God for love and mercy and one, last, final, bleeding Sacrifice! Thank God for the message of deliverance we have to preach! Anything less is not worthy of being called gospel.

Dr. Christiaan Barnard tells of one of his heart-transplant patients asking to see the removed organ. Obligingly, the doctor brought from the laboratory the large bottle which contained the old heart. As the man looked at the big muscle which once pumped life through his body, the famed surgeon suddenly realized that this was the first time in human experience that a person had ever seen his own heart. It was indeed a historic moment. But for the patient the sensation must have been even more moving, for the old heart was worn out. Had it not been replaced, life would soon have been extinct. After a long pause, the grateful man looked up and said, "I'm glad I don't have that old heart anymore."[32]

This is our wonderful message! No one needs to have that old heart anymore. It is eternally relevant. It is not always men's perceived need, but it is always at the base of actual need.

Man's worst was the world's greatest tragedy — sin, rebellion, the Fall, and all it brought with it.

God's best is atonement — a loving Father, a beloved Son, a bleeding sacrifice, a way of restoration opened.

Know it, experience it, preach it, and lead others to it. God will permit us to do no less.

Notes

1. *The Discipline of The Wesleyan Church,* 1976 (Marion, Indiana: The Wesleyan Publishing House, 1976), p. 22. Also see Genesis 8:21; Psalm 51:5; Jeremiah 17:9; Mark 7:21-23; Romans 3:10-12, 5:12,18-19; Ephesians 2:1-3.
2. Ibid., p. 22. Also see Luke 24:46-47; John 3:16; Acts 3:18; 4:12; Romans 5:8-11,18-19; 8:34; I Corinthians 6:11; 15:22; Galatians 2:16; 3:2-3; Ephesians 1:7; 2:13,16; I Timothy 2:5-6; Hebrews 7:23-27; 9:11-15,24-28; 10:14.
3. Merne A. Harris and Richard S. Taylor, "The Dual Nature of Sin," compiled by Kenneth E. Geiger, *The Word and The Doctrine* (Kansas City, Missouri: Beacon Hill Press, 1965), p. 91.
4. H. Orton Wiley, S.T.D., *Christian Theology* (Kansas City, Missouri: Nazarene Publishing House, 1941), Vol. II, p. 51.
5. Genesis 3:6
6. Romans 5:12-21; I Corinthians 15:45ff.
7. J. Kenneth Grider, "The Origin of Sin: Initially," Geiger, op. cit., p. 76.
8. Mendell Taylor, *Exploring Evangelism* (Kansas City, Missouri: Nazarene Publishing House, 1964), p. 586.
9. See Carlyle Marney, *Faith in Conflict* (New York: Abingdon Press, 1957), p. 48.
10. Grider, op. cit., p. 70.

11. Donald S. Metz, *Studies in Biblical Holiness* (Kansas City, Missouri: Beacon Hill Press of Kansas City, 1971), pp. 52,53.
12. Wiley, op. cit., p. 102.
13. James 4:17
14. Grider, op. cit., p. 76.
15. W. T. Purkiser, Ph.D., Richard S. Taylor, Ph.D., and Willard H. Taylor, Ph.D., *God, Man, & Salvation* (Kansas City, Missouri: Beacon Hill Press of Kansas City, 1977), p. 87.
16. Romans 7:21
17. Ephesians 2:1
18. *Discipline,* op. cit., p. 22.
19. Romans 12:11
20. Matthew 26:28
21. John 3:16
22. Romans 1:18
23. Mark 15:34
24. Isaiah 59:2
25. Purkiser, Taylor, and Taylor, op. cit., pp. 400,401.
26. Robert E. Coleman, quoting from *Coronet,* in *Written in Blood* (Old Tappan, New Jersey: Fleming H. Revell Company, 1972), p. 32.
27. W. A. Criswell, *What a Saviour* (Nashville, Tennessee: Broadman Press, 1978), quoted in *Christian Review,* October 1978.
28. *Discipline,* op. cit., p. 22.
29. Coleman, op. cit., p. 26.
30. William Arnett, "The Nature and Extent of the Atonement," Geiger, op. cit., p. 170.
31. Metz, op. cit., p. 9.
32. Coleman, op. cit., p. 17.

The Nature of Justification

3

Virgil A. Mitchell

God's provision for man's salvation concerns the past, the present, and the future. We are told in Hebrews 9:11-12, "Christ . . . by his own blood . . . obtained eternal redemption for us." It happened on a cross at Calvary. Also the present process of redemption is in full force. We read in Titus 2:11-14, "For the grace of God that bringeth salvation hath appeared to all men, teaching us that, denying ungodliness and worldly lusts, we should live soberly, righteously, and godly, in this present world; looking for that blessed hope, and the glorious appearing of the great God and our Saviour Jesus Christ; who gave himself for us, that he might redeem us from all iniquity, and purify unto himself a peculiar people. . . ." Salvation has been provided and is now available to all. Likewise, the prospective plan for future realization is unfolding before us. It is described in Ephesians 4:30 as being "sealed by the Holy Spirit unto the day of redemption"; in Romans 8:23 as "waiting for . . . the redemption of our body"; and in Luke 21:28 as eagerly looking for the second coming of Christ because with that event "our redemption draweth nigh." These aspects of redemption shall be accomplished through justification, regeneration, entire sanctification, and glorification. This study shall be confined to justification in its inclusive meaning embracing justification, regeneration, adoption, and related questions of good works and sin after justification.

The Meaning of Justification

The Wesleyan Church has defined the meaning of justification and its related questions in its Articles of Religion XI, XII, XIII, and XIV.

> Article XI. Justification of Man
>
> We are accounted righteous before God only for the merit of our Lord and Saviour Jesus Christ, by faith, and not for our own works or deservings. Wherefore, that we are justified by faith only is a most wholesome doctrine, and very full of comfort.
>
> Acts 13:38-39; 15:11; 16:31; Rom. 3:28; 4:2-5; 5:1-2; Eph. 2:8-9; Phil. 3:9; Heb. 11.

Justification means to be declared or accounted righteous just as if one had never been unrighteous. This does not merely involve an imputed righteousness but an imparted righteousness as well. This accounting of one to be righteous is based upon the full payment of the penalty of a broken law and the full pardon for the one who broke that law. Man was guilty of the broken law. Christ paid that penalty. Not only is man declared righteous upon believing or accepting the merit of Christ's death; he is made righteous by the blood of Christ and, from that moment, growth in grace and increase in righteousness become not only his privilege but his responsibility.

Justification is closely related to, but is distinct from, regeneration and adoption. The new birth produces three great changes:

1. Justification — a change of record in relation to the violation of God's divine law.
2. Regeneration — a change of moral character and the renewal of the fallen nature.
3. Adoption — a change of relationship restoring

sonship and constituting the penitent, believing sinner a child of God.

Experientially justification, regeneration, and adoption take place simultaneously by one and the same act of faith, each being one aspect of becoming a child of God. The Lord never justifies or pardons a sinner without renewing him. He never regenerates or changes one's moral character without adopting or restoring him to sonship. The removal of guilt in justification, the renewal of spiritual life in the soul in regeneration, and the restoration of sonship in adoption constitute the process by which one is converted, becomes a Christian, receives Christ, is born again.

Article XII. Good Works

Although good works, which are the fruit of faith and follow after justification, cannot put away our sins and endure the severity of God's judgment, yet they are pleasing and acceptable to God in Christ, and spring out of a true and lively faith, insomuch that by them a lively faith may be as evidently known as a tree is discerned by its fruit.

Matt. 5:16; 7:16-20; John 15:8; Rom. 3:20; 4:2,4,6; Gal. 2:16; Phil. 1:11; Titus 3:5; James 2:18,22; I Peter 2:9,12.

Our Article on Good Works was aimed at two serious fallacies:

1. Those who believed they merited salvation on the basis of their good works.
2. Those who de-emphasize the place of works in the Christian life leading to antinomianism which disclaimed any responsibility to keep the moral law because they claimed grace made it unnecessary.

Common terms used to describe these fallacies were "salvation by works" and "sinning religion." Present-day legalism and prevalent antinomianism have their roots in these misconceptions.

Good works do not merit salvation; they are the fruit of salvation. Wherever there is genuine faith, it will manifest itself like fruit on a tree indicating there is inward life in the tree. To keep good works in proper perspective

both prior to and following justification has concerned Christians for countless years. That salvation is earned from works; that a superior level of grace can be accumulated by good works; and that ignoring ethical and moral responsibilities because good works were thought to supersede grace led to the following abuses:
1. Bringing into the church unconverted and uncommitted members.
2. Selling of indulgences and later to unwholesome legalism.
3. Professing religion that condoned evil and demonstrated a low standard of grace.

We are saved by grace, through faith and not by works, but real faith works because faith touches the totality of a person — his intellect, heart, and will. Man can never accumulate extra merit by works because Jesus declared: "When ye shall have done all those things which are commanded you, say, We are unprofitable servants: we have done that which was our duty to do" (Luke 17:10).

Article XIII. Sin After Justification

Not every sin willfully committed after justification is the sin against the Holy Spirit and unpardonable (Matthew 12:31-32). Wherefore, the grant of repentance is not to be denied to such as fall into sin after justification. After we have received this grace, we may depart therefrom and fall into sin, and by the grace of God rise again and amend our lives. Therefore, they are to be condemned who say they can no more sin as long as they live here, or deny the place of forgiveness to such as truly repent (Malachi 3:7; Matthew 18:21-22; I John 1:9; 2:1).

This Article recognizes the possibility of Christians committing sin; the serious consequences resulting from those sins; and that — through the grace of God — forgiveness, restoration, and amendment of life are possible. Originally this teaching was aimed primarily to those who taught that every sin committed after justification was the sin of blasphemy against the Holy Ghost for which no forgiveness was possible. Readmittance to church membership was denied those who fell into sin. Others claimed a kind of "protective shield" within the covenant of grace that made it impossible to sin. However, this Article speaks appropriately to this permissive generation that one "may depart from grace" but it is not the norm or habit of Christians. If one should fall into sin, he may turn to God in repentance and faith to find forgiveness and restoration (I John 2:12). Sin is a serious matter. It may lead to blasphemy against the Holy Spirit (Matthew 12:31-32). This is no ordinary sin. It is a deliberate, obstinate, persistent rejection of Jesus Christ. "It is unpardonable," declared Hilary T. Hudson, "not because God withholds mercy to any truly penitent, but because all such have reached such a state of moral desperation that they will not ask or receive pardon on the conditions of the gospel. The unpardonable state is in the man, not in the unwillingness of God to forgive."

Article XIV. Regeneration

Regeneration is that work of the Holy Spirit by which the pardoned sinner becomes a child of God; this work is received through faith in Jesus Christ, whereby the regenerate are delivered from the power of sin which reigns over all the unregenerate, so that they love God and through grace serve Him with the will and affections of the heart — receiving "the Spirit of adoption, whereby we cry, Abba, Father."

John 1:12-13; 3:3,5; Rom. 8:15,17; Gal. 3:26; 4:5,7; Eph. 1:5; 2:5,19; 4:24; Col. 3:10; Titus 3:5; James 1:18; I Peter 1:3-4; II Peter 1:4; I John 3:1.

The root meaning of the compound word "re" and "generation" is to "make over, to form again, or to restore again after having lost its original shape, relation, position, or character." It presupposes degeneration, wreckage, lostness.

In a theological or biblical sense it means restoration of spiritual life in the soul of one who was dead in trespasses and sin (Ephesians 2:1-22). It is correctly called "the moral miracle of redemption" which provides pardon, forgiveness, and reconciliation for penitent sinners. It is the re-creation of spiritual life in the soul, not merely a patchwork of repairs or the replacement of a few worn-out parts in the moral character of mankind (II Corinthians 5:17; Galatians 6:15). Regeneration is recovery from the terrible lost estate of sin; it is a complete renovation of the depraved moral character; it is reconciliation from a great gulf of alienation between sinful man and a holy God caused by the fall of Adam; and it is restoration of sonship which man surrendered by rejecting the claims of God upon his life when he willfully partook of the forbidden fruit in the garden.

Regeneration is related to yet different from justification. Justification is what God does for us; regeneration is what God does in us. Justification removes the guilt of sin; regeneration provides washing or cleansing of acquired depravity. This is initial sanctification. Inherited depravity or original birth sin is removed in entire sanctification. Justification brings a change of state; regeneration brings a change of nature. Justification removes the punishment we deserve and remits the penalty of the broken law; regeneration imparts the moral principle of love and obedience in the heart. Pardon takes away guilt, removes moral evil, and places one in the kingdom of God. It is attested to by the witness of the Holy Spirit. It is retained by habitual submission, unwavering trust, and unquestioned obedience to all that God requires.

The Bible declares: "The law of the Lord is perfect, converting the soul" (Psalm 19:7). "Except ye be converted, and become as little children, ye shall not enter into the kingdom of heaven" (Matthew 18:3). "Except a man be born again, he cannot see the kingdom of God" (John 3:3). "Therefore being justified by faith, we have peace with God through our Lord Jesus Christ" (Romans 5:1). "Therefore if any man be in Christ, he is a new creature: old things are passed away; behold, all things are become new" (II Corinthians 5:17).

Recovery of the lost, deliverance from bondage, transformation from the kingdom of Satan to the kingdom of God, forgiveness of sins, and being born again are scriptural terms used to describe the work of regeneration. "It is a supernatural work of divine grace" (John 1:13; James 1:18; Titus 3:5). It is not merely a reformation, though reformation follows as a result of it. It is a change of allegiance. Self and Satan are dethroned. Christ is enthroned within, a new direction is given to the will.

The necessity and importance of regeneration cannot be overestimated. Those who personally receive this transforming experience find that love, joy, and peace fill their hearts; righteousness governs their conduct; and the hope of heaven impels them onward in their quest for more of the grace of God. This is life at its best! Conversely, those who fail to have this question answered not only rob themselves of a highly satisfactory life here on earth, but they deny themselves an eternal home in heaven hereafter.

The most common term used today to define regeneration is "born again." It is a term to which a vast majority of people can relate. According to a recent Gallup poll, one-third of the American people profess to be born-again Christians. It has become a "household word" as a result of the well-publicized presidential campaign of "born-again candidates" in the United States in 1976. The conversion of Charles Colson of the Watergate scandal and the subsequent book and movie, *Born Again,* has given an added dimension to this phrase. It is perhaps easier than ever to talk about this experience. However, the common and careless usage of the phrase poses a concern. Its true meaning is being debased by its popular usage. The news media are applying "born again" to such items as a "born-again stock market" which recovered from a heavy loss; and to the "born-again Muhammad Ali" who regained his heavyweight boxing title from Leon

Spinks. The draining of the meaning of language has been with us for a long time. It once was good soul-winning strategy to inquire, "Are you a Christian?" The abuse of the word "Christian" made this approach counterproductive. Most everyone who did not consider himself to be a pagan replied affirmatively. A better approach became to inquire. "Are you a 'born-again' Christian?" The true meaning of being born again must be fully communicated and properly utilized in order to secure genuine conversion and to keep alive the dynamic witness of the need for and the meaning of this transforming relationship which Christ provides. Therefore, other biblical terminology must be associated with our use of the words "born again."

The Means by Which Justification Is Obtained

Justification is available to all — without regard to race, culture, position, or standing — on terms or conditions that all can meet. These conditions are:

1. Respond to God's Initiative for Your Salvation

"Christ died for our sins . . was buried, and . . . rose again the third day . . ." (I Corinthians 15:3-4).

The depth of sin infected the totality of man's being. Left to himself, man could never redeem himself. God's prevenient grace — "the unconditional benefit of the atonement" — enables man to respond to the call of God, to heed the invitation of Christ, to yield to the wooing of the Holy Spirit, and through the influence of the Holy Spirit to exercise saving faith for salvation. The Holy Spirit convicts (reproves) of sin. He strives and pleads for man to be born again. God's invitation and offer of salvation may be ignored, frustrated, resisted, and rejected. Man may, on the other hand, heed and respond to that call. Jesus said, "*Come* unto me, all ye that labor and are heavy laden, and I will give you rest. *Take* my yoke upon you, and learn of me . . . and ye shall find rest unto your souls"

(Matthew 11:28-29). *"Seek* ye the Lord while he may be found, *call* ye upon him while he is near: Let the wicked *forsake* his way, and the unrighteous man his thoughts: and let him *return* unto the Lord, and he will have mercy upon him; and to our God, for he will abundantly pardon" (Isaiah 55:6-7). *"Put away* the evil of your doings . . . *learn* to do well. . . . *Come now,* and let us reason together, saith the Lord: though your sins be as scarlet, they shall be as white as snow; though they be red like crimson, they shall be as wool" (Isaiah 1:16-18).

The way of salvation is completed. God only awaits man's response for it to become effective in a personal sense.

2. **Repent of Your Sins**

Repentance is the beginning point into personal salvation. The imperative of repentance is mentioned at least seventy times in the New Testament. John Wesley calls, "repentance the porch, faith the door, and holiness religion itself" *(Works,* Vol. VIII). Salvation is by faith alone, but there can be no evangelical faith apart from genuine repentance. One cannot exercise faith and consciously engage in sin at the same time. Faith and disobedience are not compatible. Repentance is a deep sorrow for and a turning away from sin. It is ceasing to rebel against God's will and way. It is making restitution wherein possible and proper. It is surrendering to Christ. It is a change of mind, purpose, allegiance, and direction. "Repent ye therefore, and be converted, that your sins may be blotted out . . ." (Acts 3:19). "Except ye repent, ye shall all likewise perish" (Luke 13:3). "Ye were made sorry, but . . . ye sorrowed to repentance; for ye were made sorry after a godly manner . . . for godly sorrow worketh repentance to salvation not to be repented of . . ." (II Corinthians 7:9-10). Both repentance and faith are essential to forgiveness. Jesus properly relates repentance and faith when he urges "Repent ye, and believe the gospel" (Mark 1:15).

Repentance and faith properly co-joined lead to justification, regeneration, adoption, and the witness of the Holy Spirit. An unbalanced emphasis on repentance may lead one to expect salvation by works and to equate repentance to salvation and to confuse salvation with strong emotional feelings. An unbalanced emphasis on faith may produce an "easy believism" of mere mental assent issuing into a shallow and superficial profession of religion.

The acid test of repentance, faith, and profession of religion is restitution. In the case of injury done intentionally or by accident, restitution was required by the Mosaic law (Leviticus 6:1-7). This law of restitution was based upon the justice of God and is therefore fully applicable today. We must confess if we are to be forgiven (I John 1:9); must forgive others if we are to be forgiven (Matthew 5:14-15); must leave the altar and seek reconciliation if there is wrong relationship between ourselves and others before we can properly worship (Matthew 5:23-24).

3. Receive Christ By Faith

"As many as received him, to them gave he power (the right or privilege) to become the sons of God, even to them that believe on his name: which were born, not of blood, nor of the will of the flesh, nor of the will of man, but of God" (John 1:12-13). In answering the question of the Philippian jailer, "What must I do to be saved?" Paul replied, "Believe on the Lord Jesus Christ, and thou shalt be saved" (Acts 16:30-31). This kind of faith is more than intellectual belief, more than an emotional decision. It is an act of the heart, an act of the will. "That if thou shalt confess with thy mouth the Lord Jesus, and shalt believe in thine heart that God hath raised him from the dead, thou shalt be saved. For with the heart man believeth unto righteousness; and with the mouth confession is made unto salvation" (Romans 10:9-10). True evangelical faith possesses three elements:

1. Assent of the mind, intellect, or understanding to the truth of the provisions of the atoning death of Christ on the cross.
2. The consent of the will and of the affections to God's plan of salvation without dependence on anything else.
3. Commitment and complete trust in Jesus Christ. "To cast one's whole weight upon" conveys the true idea of faith. Thus "the faith of commitment is preceded by the faith of confidence."

A great salvation has been provided. This is God's part. Respond, repent, receive — is man's part.

Marks of Justification

Man can be saved and he can know it, be certain of it. How?

The witness of the Holy Spirit in the heart of the Christian bears witness of his acceptance with God. The Scriptures declare: "For ye have not received the spirit of bondage again to fear; but ye have received the Spirit of adoption, whereby we cry, Abba, Father. The Spirit itself beareth witness with our spirit, that we are the children of God" (Romans 8:15-16). "Hereby know we that we dwell in him, and he in us, because he hath given us of his Spirit" (I John 4:13). "He that believeth on the Son of God hath the witness in himself" (I John 5:10).

It is evident that God witnesses to His acceptance of the Christian. It is a direct witness — the Holy Spirit bearing witness (testifying) with the spirit (consciousness) of the Christian and the spirit of the Christian accepting and responding to that testimony. John Wesley said: "Let none ever presume to rest in any supposed testimony of the Spirit which is separate from the fruit of it. And let none rest in any supposed fruit of the Spirit without the witness. . . . Our Maker has placed a double guard around our spiritual and eternal interest. . . . What the Spirit . . . makes evident to our consciousness, our spirit makes evident to our reason. What the former reveals by an immediate impression, the latter demonstrates by inference and argument; both unite in declaring that now are we the sons of God."

The indirect witness of the Holy Spirit gives proof that one is born again. The Holy Spirit witnesses initially, additionally, and continuously. The initial witness is direct — the Holy Spirit and my spirit testifying jointly that I am now a child of God. The additional witness is inferential — a consciousness that I have complied with the scriptural requirements for being born again and therefore God has done what He promised. The continuous witness is indirect — the presence of the fruit of the Spirit in my daily life.

The witness of the Word is indeed a strong witness but requires an absolute honesty and complete willingness to do and be all the Bible demands of a penitent sinner. "If we confess our sins, he is faithful and just to forgive us our sins, and to cleanse us from all unrighteousness" (I John 1:9). "Behold, I stand at the door, and knock: if any man hear my voice, and open the door, I will come in to him, and will sup with him, and he with me" (Revelation 3:20).

When all scriptural conditions have been fully met, then the provisions set forth therein can be clearly claimed. This is the Spirit's additional witness.

The witness of one's daily walk is a part of the complete witness of the Spirit. If one has the true witness, he will not only be a Christian in profession; he will be a Christian in practice. "But if we walk in the light, as he is in the light, we have fellowship one with another, and the blood of Jesus Christ his Son cleanseth us from all sin" (I John 1:7). "And hereby we do know that we know him, if we keep his commandments. He that saith, I know him, and keepeth not his commandments, is a liar, and the truth is not in him. But whoso keepeth his word, in him verily is the love of God perfected: hereby know we that we are in him" (I John 2:3-5). "Love not the world, neither the things that are in the world. If any man love the world, the love of the Father is not in him" (I John 2:15). "If ye know that he is righteous, ye know that every one that doeth righteousness is born of him" (I John 2:29). "We know that we have passed from death unto life, because we love the brethren. He that loveth not his brother abideth in death" (I John 3:14). "But whoso hath this world's good, and seeth his brother have need, and shutteth up his bowels of compassion from him, how dwelleth the love of God in him?" (I John 3:17). "Beloved, let us love one another: for love is of God; and everyone that loveth is born of God, and knoweth God" (I John 4:7).

Many have confessed with their lips, believed with their hearts, and demonstrated by their lives that they were truly born again. If others, why not you?

Receiving the experience of the new birth, effectively communicating the doctrine, and leading others to accept Christ are essential for renewal and revival. Knowing the doctrine will not accomplish it. We have enough knowledge to save the world if knowledge would do it. Effectively communicating that knowledge will do it. The Samaritan woman who met Christ at Jacob's well demonstrates that it can be done. Harry Denman graphically stated: "She was converted at high noon but became a soul-winner before the sun went down." A marvelous chapter indeed. What kind of chapter will we write? Time will tell!

The Nature of Sanctification

J. D. Abbott

I know of no reason why the church or her scholars should undertake to write a new definition on the subject of heart holiness or Christian perfection. As Daniel Steele once noted, that except in what may be referred to as progressive sciences where discoveries of new information are frequently made, to rewrite definitions from time to time is unnecessary.

Divergence of opinion exists on certain aspects of the doctrine and always has — doubtless, the same shall continue into the future. However, there are some items on which there is fairly common agreement: it is generally believed that man is naturally unholy. It is conceded that persons who are unholy shall have no admittance into the kingdom of heaven. It is agreed that man cannot make himself holy but, rather, only the blood of Jesus Christ is an effective remedy for the sin problem that possesses man. In line with biblical teaching, it is admitted that man must be made holy before he can be received into the presence of God. And John Wesley seemed to feel that one of the great needs of the world was to have all believers earnestly and persistently strive for the experience.

The Scripture is adequately clear in setting forth in

type and teaching that the Lord Jesus Christ undertook to do a deeper work than justification, reconciliation, and regeneration. He suffered on the cross for the purpose of sanctifying the unholy, and the Word emphasizes with dynamic force that holiness of heart and life are as important and necessary as are justification and regeneration through the shedding of the blood of Jesus Christ.

The Holy Spirit is faithful in the whole process of redemption — to convict us of sins and our lost estate, as well as to bring us to an understanding of the nature of sin which possesses us and from which we long and sigh for full deliverance.

Dr. William S. Deal sees the truth and experience of entire sanctification, or Christian holiness, as being the greatest legacy of God's people. He notes that from the foundation of the world God has proposed that man, His created creature, should be holy and without blame in the world. Beyond that, he highlights the fact that this heritage is for every believer in the Lord Jesus Christ — emphasizing that the experience is not for sinners but, rather, is to be entered into after a sinner is saved by grace. In addition, it is noted that God's highest will is emphasized through the doctrine of heart purity, and man's attention is drawn to the holiness of God, being reminded that God wants the same of His creatures as is His undefiled nature.

The Meaning It Embodies

When Dr. J. B. Chapman was asked to explain what is meant by being wholly sanctified and how one may know he has that grace, he said: "Wholly sanctified is not strictly speaking a Scriptural term. But it is an expression necessary to bear the thought contained in I Thessalonians 5:23, 'The very God of peace sanctify you wholly; and I pray your whole spirit and soul and body be preserved blameless unto the coming of our Lord Jesus Christ.' And the next verse says, 'Faithful is he that calleth you, who also will do it.' When one is truly converted or born again, he is initially or partially sanctified, for he is cleansed from the guilt of sin. But there yet remains within him that 'prone to wander,' that 'bent to iniquity,' that 'sin that so easily besets,' that 'depravity of nature' with which we are all born and which is the root of sin as action, and from which the gospel promises deliverance. If any ask why this was not also cleansed away at the time of conversion, I would answer, for one reason, because the conditions upon which cleansing is promised cannot be met until one has been born again. But God has provided this full cleansing in the blood of Jesus Christ (Hebrews 13:12; I John 1:8). Its condition is faith, and its executor is the Holy Spirit. And since this blessing is invariably received after regeneration, John Wesley spoke of it as 'the second blessing properly so-called.' It is sought in prayer, and it is to be instantaneously wrought whenever the consecrated Christian believes fully for God to do it."

Therefore, the prayer of the apostle as given above was a prayer that all of the powers and temperaments and constitution of our being would be purified from all that is unholy and, in addition, fully sanctified and devoted to the Lord Jesus Christ. It is nothing less than the consecration of the Christian's whole being to the Lord Jesus Christ and the subjection of his total person to the control of one principle — that being faith in the Son of God.

When John Fletcher was writing on the subject of Christian perfection, he explained it as follows: "We mean nothing but the cluster and maturity of the graces which compose the Christian character in the church militant. In other words, Christian perfection is a spiritual constellation made up of those gracious stars — perfect dependence, perfect faith, perfect humility, perfect meekness, perfect self-denial, perfect resignation, perfect hope, perfect charity for our physical enemies as well as for our earthly relations; and above all, perfect love for our invisible God to the explicit knowledge of our mediator, Jesus Christ; and as this last star is always accompanied by all the others, as Jupiter is by his satellites, we frequently use the phrase perfect love instead of perfection, understanding by it the pure love of God shed abroad in the hearts of established believers by the Holy Ghost, which is abundantly given them under the fullness of the Christian dispensation."

In the sixty or more years that John Wesley gave to thinking and writing on holiness, he defined it by various methods but most often used the term of love — saying that it involved loving God with all of our heart and serving Him with all of our strength.

He went on to say that entire sanctification was, in fact, neither more nor less than pure love. It was a love that expelled sin and governed the heart and the life of the child of God. He advised various Christians to frequently read and think upon the message borne in the thirteenth chapter of the first epistle to the Corinthians, saying that here is the true picture of Christian perfection, and urged everyone to copy after it with all sincerity.

When some of those who followed him intently became a little confused at some point, he invariably called them back to this understanding of love. In fact, he wrote to Lawrence Coughlan saying, "You never learned, either from my conversation or preaching or writings, that 'holiness consisted in a flow of joy.' I constantly told you quite the contrary: I told you it was love; the love of God and our neighbor; the image of God stamped on the heart; the life of God in the soul of man; the mind that was in Christ, enabling us to walk as Christ also walked."

Numerous clauses, phrases, and figures of speech have been employed to set forth the meaning of sanctification, such as — the consecration of our whole being to Christ; the perfect assimilation of our entire character to that of Christ; the perpetual employment of all our powers in His service; one desire and design ruling all our tempers, devoting all our soul, body, and substance to God; the circumcision of the heart from all filthiness, from all inward as well as outward pollution; and the renewal of the heart in the image of God.

It consists of the two ideas of separation and consecration — separation from the world and devotement to God. To be sanctified is to be made holy, to be cleansed from sin.

The Reverend S. G. Rhoads put it like this: "To be wholly sanctified means to be saved from all sin; to be pure in heart; to enjoy such a state of Christian experience as to be entirely separated from the world and redeemed from every stain and pollution of sin; so that we live no longer to ourselves, but are wholly consecrated to the service of God." He went on to say, "The doctrine of sanctification, or holiness, is a central idea of revealed religion, that is, therefore, of superior importance. The necessity of holiness is prominently set forth in the Old and New Testaments."

In Exodus 19:6 we read: "And ye shall be unto me a kingdom of priests, and a holy nation."

In Leviticus 11:44 we read: "For I am the Lord your God: ye shall therefore sanctify yourselves, and ye shall be holy; for I am holy."

In II Corinthians 7:1 we note the words: "Having therefore these promises, dearly beloved, let us cleanse ourselves from all filthiness of the flesh and spirit, perfecting holiness in the fear of God."

Also, I Thessalonians 4:3 should be noted: "For this is the will of God, even your sanctification." And as well, Hebrews 12:14, "Follow peace with all men, and holiness, without which no man shall see the Lord."

This message has had a long and unbroken history in the life of the Christian church. It has contributed to the devotional life of the church and, at the same time, been the subject of great controversy among theologians. Its message is both attractive and challenging. It is a fact that we delight in the enjoyments of a perfect evening, in the sight of a perfect rose; but when we make reference to a perfect soul or a moral nature that is perfect, our tender spirits seem to faint as if to say it is a total impossibility.

The Need It Reveals

The problem within the breast of man is described by the use of many figures: original sin, indwelling sin, moral depravity, remains of the carnal mind, and other similar terms. However, whatever terminology is used, it is a fact, undeniable, that there remains in the believer, after his conversion, that which withstands the purposes of God, leaving the individual unfit to dwell in the presence of His everlasting holiness. However, there is a fountain provided for the cleansing from all pollution, and every believer may plunge therein. In that fountain believers may be washed from all the impurities of sin and cleansed from all the filthiness of the flesh and spirit and redeemed from every affection and desire which is contrary to the law and will of God.

The need that is revealed in God's dealings with man makes reference to a "former conversation," the "old man," a "corruption according to deceitful lust." A reference is made to a weight that besets us which must be laid aside. The divine requirement is made clear that God's people shall be kept unspotted from the world, and the truth is forthrightly spoken that the unclean person shall have no inheritance in the kingdom of Christ and of God.

Dr. Leslie D. Wilcox believes that the best illustration of the need, and the divine ministry with reference to that need, may be to draw a parallel between a carnal soul and a body which is subject to some kind of infection. He says, "The infection is not the presence of a foreign body in the physical system. It may produce physical manifestations, but the infection itself is simply a wrong condition of the physical system. This infection can be removed."

The need that the unsanctified believer experiences is one that refers to the pollution and the power of sin.

The Nature with Which It Deals

Dr. George Allen Turner in *The Vision Which Transforms* notes that "the concept of holiness or perfection cannot be adequately grasped apart from a familiarity with the concept of sin. The church has always regarded sin as having a twofold character; that of individual acts, and also of disposition which prompts evil acts. It is this second aspect of sin, that of an evil principle, which, if found in the New Testament, is the more pertinent to this day."

Dr. Turner goes on to note that Paul's idea of the nature of sin could be summarized as follows: "(1) sin inheres in the flesh as a foreign, alienable, and therefore separable element; (2) this indwelling sin exists in the justified person; (3) this indwelling sin may and must be separated from human nature by the indwelling Spirit of Christ."

And so, original sin should not be seen to be so much guilt for Adam's transgression as a sinful condition which stems from that transgression.

Sin is seen to be a unit, that is, the nature of sin is such that where one of its attributes appears, every other attribute is inherently present — even the body of sin itself. So, if there is one carnal manifestation in the soul, all the rest are there, though they may lie dormant for the time being and possibly will never show themselves. But inbred sin must be removed. It manifests itself in ways that are not pleasing to God — in pride, envy, jealousy, lust, and the like. It is not the casting out of one of these that is so important but, rather, the very nature must be dealt with — the nature from which these issue.

The Purpose It Fulfills

The inward corruption is cleansed away, the work of purification is completed, and the washed soul is kept clean.

The purpose of God in sending His Son into the world was to "destroy the works of the devil" (I John 3:8), and to "save his people from their sins" (Matthew 1:21). In addition, God — through Christ — proposed to "redeem us from all iniquity, and purify unto himself a peculiar people, zealous of good works" (Titus 2:14).

L. L. Pickett in his book, *The Book and Its Theme,* gives a beautiful expression to this subject. He wrote, "Bible is simply 'book' but the mission of the Book is expressed in the qualifying word 'holy'; hence, 'Holy Book' — that is, a book to teach holiness. The theme of grammar is 'the science of language'; the theme of arithmetic is 'the science of numbers'; and the theme of the Bible is the science of holiness. As grammar has no other mission than that of teaching the correct use of language; as the dictionary is only to teach the correct spelling, pronunciation, and definition of words; as history is to teach the doings and movements of men and nations in the past, so the Bible is to teach us of man's creation in the image of God, of his sad fall by sin, and of the means of his restoration to the divine image and the life of holiness that he may be prepared to enter into a holy heaven after his life's work is done." In this we see that the "Holy Book" is a vehicle employed by God to accomplish His purposes in the hearts of men, namely, to restore them to the divine image.

It is clearly God's purpose that man experience an entire separation from sin and a purification by the blood of Christ from all evil affections and desires.

It is God's purpose for man to be filled, spirit, soul, and body, with the love of God, which will inspire and excite his whole being for the service of the Saviour. It is God's purpose for man's mind, will, and affections to be governed by the Holy Spirit so that his life is wholly lived in God and God in him.

It is God's purpose for man to have a godly walk and conversation, for him to follow Christ — not imaginarily, but in reality, doing and suffering the will of God even as He did.

It is God's purpose that our bodies be preserved blameless — that does not free us from fatigue or disease or death. That does not imply that there shall be no desire excited through physical propensity. But He would have us preserved in a sanctified and blameless state with all of our being held in perfect and perpetual subjection to the will of God. God's objective is that we shall be a perfect reflection of those things that are true and honest and just and pure and lovely and of good report.

God proposes that we shall, in the sanctified state, be blameless in regard to our wills, blameless in every choice, blameless in every preference, and blameless in every volition. He would have our perpetual language to be, "Lord, what wilt thou have me do?"

The Benefits It Bestows

The sanctified life is one that is enriched by reason of the experience of heart cleansing. It is enriched with patience and kindness and all the other Christian graces.

The sanctified life is one of moral beauty. It reflects the beauty of the face of God and of the character of God. The sanctified soul is one that is lit up by divine glory — a reflection of the glory of God in the face of Jesus Christ.

When God performs the spiritual work that needs to be done in the heart of the individual, when God by His own surgical act cuts away the corruptions of sin and selfishness and fills it with His presence and possesses it as His habitation, guilt of conscience is gone and inner peace and quietness of soul exist.

The sanctified man is kept in perfect peace and rest of spirit. J. A. Wood gave a rather imposing list of the various phases of the rest of the soul. Among them are: "It is a state of settled and complete satisfaction in God, he being 'all in all' to the soul. It is a state of rest from the former servitude to doubts, fears, and inbred sin. It is a state of rest in which the tumult of the heart has been hushed in the calmness; and fear and discord and doubt have given place to quietness and assurance. It is a state of deep and permanent quietude and assurance in respect to all our interests, temporal and eternal. It is a state of sweet rest from all conflict between the will and the conscience."

Another benefit that comes with the sanctified life is the purity of life and character manifested by honesty and truthfulness and integrity and conscientiousness that it brings.

These and so many other benefits are derived by those who enter into the experience of the sanctified life.

The Source to Which It Traces

Our sanctification is of God; it is founded in His being and will, and He is its source. His Word commands it and teaches what it is. Christ, by His sacrificial death and His resurrection and glorification, is the meritorious and mediatorial cause and the author of our sanctification. In His life upon earth, He set before us a real, lifelike, and perfect model of that holiness to which we, His followers, are called according to the will of God. Our sanctification is wrought and established in us in divine reality by the Holy Spirit, who fills us with the life, and light, and love of God.

A. Paget Wilkes in *The Dynamic of Redemption* points out that the death of Christ on the cross destroys the body of sin, the blood of Christ cleanses the heart from sin, and the sufferings of Christ heal the soul.

With reference to the work of the Holy Spirit in effecting sanctification, Dr. Leslie Wilcox in *Be Ye Holy* highlights the various ministries of the Holy Spirit and illustrates those differences as follows: A young woman might receive a young man as a guest in her home. She might later receive him as her fiance, and still later receive him as her husband. In each circumstance she received the same person but in a different relationship. It could not properly be said at the first meeting, when she received a guest, that she received a husband, even though it was the man who eventually became her husband. This illustrates how there may be successive receivings of the Spirit in the life of an individual. The meaning of each experience is to be determined by the capacity in which the Spirit was received.

The Experience It Furnishes

Bishop Joseph Long in 1869 saw the experience of sanctification as a person's entire release of his will to the will of God and the living of life in such a manner that he offered up his soul with all of its powers as an offering of love to the Saviour.

The Reverend H. A. Baldwin wrote that "holiness of heart does not consist in wonderful ecstasies and raptures, but in a heart in tune with the pure love of God; not in wonderful upliftings so much as in wonderful downsinkings; not in wonderful witnesses, unless as they are accompanied with and followed by an absence of sinful tendencies; not in spiritual exultations, but in ever-deepening self-effacement. As the individual views himself and his efforts, holiness does not necessarily consist in the fact that he sees the mighty power of God working through him, but in a deep sense of his own weakness and utter dependence upon God."

Luther Lee noted that "the power of sin is broken, the

tyrant is dethroned, and his reign ceases in the soul at the moment of regeneration; yet, sin is not so destroyed as not to leave his mark upon the soul, and even yet struggle for the mastery.

"There is still a warfare within, and however clear the intellect may be to see what is right, and however determined the will may be to execute the decision of the judgment, there will be found an opposing element in the sensibility of the soul, which, though it no longer controls the will, often rebels against it and refuses to obey it. That depravity does not lie exclusively in the will, but also in the perverted passions and appetites it is too plain to be denied, and that these struggle for unlawful indulgence after regeneration is too universal in Christian experience to need proof. This state of things, as a matter of fact, must be admitted by all, yet theologians explain it in the light of their different creeds and different systems of philosophy. Hence some call it the remains of original sin, some call it indwelling sin, and some say it is the depravity that remains after regeneration." But whatever the definition or the terms that are used, it is a fact that the experience of the sanctified is an experience of release from the nature of sin that dwells within man and perverts his good purposes Godward.

The sanctified soul enjoys the experience of being clear before the omniscient eye of God. He enjoys a heavenly conversation; he forgets those things which are behind; he presses forward for the crown of life; he shines as a light in the world; he is possessed of that perfect love which casteth out all fear — the fear that hath torment. Though he is still on probation and still must fight the good fight of faith and still must suffer with Christ, yet, he shall in the end be more than a conqueror through Him who loved him. Oh, what a blessed state. The impurities of sin are taken away. The sinful affections and desires are destroyed and the powers of the soul are brought into harmony with God's will.

He rejoices in the realization that he has a deep abhorrence of the evil offered in temptation. He rejoices in a conscious absence of the inward struggles of the sinful disposition when tempted. He rejoices in the knowledge that he is clean.

He rejoices in the experience suggested in Psalm 51:6, "Thou desirest truth in the inward parts: and in the hidden part thou shalt make me to know wisdom."

He rejoices that he is preserved blameless, not meaning that he never thinks of what is evil but, rather, he rejoices in the fact that he is constantly employed in seeking to know and to perform the truth and the will of God and is constantly employed in those things that are true, honest, and of good report. He has found the more excellent way.

The Traits It Exhibits

This is so beautifully expressed by George W. Ridout in *Amazing Grace*. He put it this way: "Sanctified grace is the greatest treasure with which the soul can be enriched — a treasure in comparison with which all else is valueless. It is that grace by which the soul comes into possession of faith like Abraham, patience like Job, hope like Moses, perseverance like Noah, meekness like David, temperance like Daniel, prayerfulness like Elijah, unworldliness like James, boldness like Peter, love like John, guilelessness like Nathaniel, devotion to God and to Jesus like Paul. It is that grace which will let you sing in trial like Paul and Silas, help you to pray out of prison like Peter, keep you in the hottest fire of affliction like the three Hebrew children. Sanctification is a supernatural grace because it takes supernatural power to arrest, to control, to destroy. Sanctification is an habitual grace. Holiness becomes a habit on earth; here the saints do on earth as they do in heaven."

The traits of the sanctified include humility and the

freedom from jealousy, the grace of meekness and gentleness, the characteristic of being teachable as well as easily entreated. It is not identified as being loud and boisterous but in giving evidence of possessing a meek and quiet spirit. It does not seek to show itself in the ability to lead but in its willingness to be led; not in the ability to hold to and win a point in debate but in the ability to yield to one another and to do so with love and in kindness.

These and many other worthy traits are manifest in the sanctified life.

The Growth It Fosters

It would be unsafe for anyone to say that he now loves God with the greatest intensity he shall ever love Him, or that he has advanced to the highest experience of faithfulness and earnestness in service that he shall ever attain. To say that holiness is perfect is not to say that improvements and advancements are not made beyond the initial experience. Our love in each successive moment must correspond with our understanding, our capabilities, the increase of our knowledge, and the improvement of our understanding.

In this life we are limited by lack of knowledge and discernment, by depleted energy and physical handicaps. These limitations have considerable influence upon the extent of our service — its efficiency and effectiveness.

Asa Mahan refers to the child, saying that it is perfect as it exercises a filial and affectionate obedience to what is required within the limits of its abilities.

He refers to the man, saying that he is perfect in holiness when he gives to God the loving obedience required according to the extent of his knowledge and strength.

Day by day there may be divine bestowments or fuller acquirements that are gained by exercise and practice.

Sanctifying grace, says Ridout, is that by which the soul enjoys God, abounds in His love, and becomes more and more like Him — like Him in love, like Him in humility, in sinlessness, in purity, and in holiness.

The reasonable, loving father never requires his child at ten years of age to accomplish the work expected of an adult who has reached thirty years. Likewise, our Heavenly Father never expects us to do beyond that for which we are qualified or capable. He is pleased, however, when we with humility obey Him according to the light we presently enjoy.

There will be further growth as we walk with the Lord. The warfare within is ended. We are led in the pathway of holiness. We enjoy increased knowledge and obtain a clearer and higher view of our duty and destiny. As we do, we are enabled to better serve God's eternal purposes.

The Assurance It Inspires

How blessed the experience which sanctifying grace effects in the life of the believing Christian! There is the assurance of eternal salvation which is dependent, of course, upon his continuing commitment to and faithful service for the Lord Jesus Christ. Possessed with this, the soul can rest in its Christ with the inner persuasion that the God who loved and gave, and the Christ who responded in sacrifice has procured the redemption that is adequate and trustworthy.

How valuable it is to be absolutely certain in a matter so important as our eternal salvation. In this God has not left us in darkness. Paul unhesitatingly said, "I know" — a word oft repeated which furnishes the groundwork of glad assurance that is found throughout his epistles.

Assurance is a term that is exceptionally rich in spiritual meaning. It signifies the joyous, unwavering confidence of an intelligent faith and the security of an unshrinking trust. It is at the very heart of vital salvation. It is the soul's experience of freedom from the power of sin and from judgment through the atoning grace of Christ.

Assurance is both a wonderful and gracious arrangement in the plan of our redemption so that we may know beyond a doubt that we are the children of God. To know that our names are written in heaven is of greatest value according to Jesus' own statement to the seventy. He said, "Rejoice not because the spirits obey you: rejoice because your names are enrolled in heaven" (Luke 10:20, Moffatt). This is a double assurance — the Spirit himself beareth witness with the believer's spirit that he is a child of God and that his name is inscribed in the book of life. This blessed assurance puts the soul quite out of taste with many other things. It is a mental and spiritual confidence of sins forgiven, of justification before God, and of heart cleansing by the blood of Christ — it is a glad sense of security, of freedom, and of eternal life in Him.

Fanny Crosby caught this truth in her own spirit when she wrote those well-known and comforting lines:

Blessed assurance, Jesus is mine!
Oh, what a foretaste of glory divine!
Heir of salvation, purchase of God,
Born of his Spirit, washed in his blood.

Perfect submission, perfect delight,
Visions of rapture now burst on my sight;
Angels, descending, bring from above,
Echoes of mercy, whispers of love.

Perfect submission, all is at rest,
I in my Saviour am happy and blest;
Watching and waiting, looking above,
Filled with his goodness, lost in his love.

Conclusion

Sanctification is a biblical truth. Its blessings are manifold. It enables us to walk in the full light of God's countenance and provides a clear witness of being saved from inbred sin. It is not a private theory or merely a denominational teaching but, rather, the Bible's own statement. The need for this spiritual work, this dynamic cleansing, is universal. The word must be declared as far as the need is found. Every available resource and opportunity must be used to preach and promote this truth.

Henry Fisher wrote in 1849: "The doctrine of holiness, or entire sanctification, ought to be at all times our chief topic, because it is the top, as well as the cornerstone of Christianity. It is the substance of Christian experience, and the heart of the religion of Jesus Christ. Take away the doctrine of full redemption, and its being ready and offered today and now, and the salt will have lost its savor, and God's dear children will be destitute of that food which their Heavenly Father has provided for them in the gospel. Every minister of the gospel should try to hold forth this doctrine in its purity. Every believer ought to use his utmost endeavors to come up to the standard of Christian perfection. Since this is the doctrine of our Church and of the Bible, we should be firm and immovable, recommend it by example and precept wherever we are, and, trusting in the Lord, stand as men of courage in its defense."

Holiness is of such moment to every follower of the Lord Jesus Christ that it is difficult to imagine that any of them would not rejoice at every effort that's put forth for its promotion.

Luther Lee in his *Elements of Theology* says, "No question in theology is of greater practical importance to every Christian than the doctrine of sanctification." It is to this truth, it is to this ministry, it is to this experience that The Wesleyan Church is committed, and it carries the message wherever it serves with the prayer in its heart and on its lips that many believers shall be brought into the experience of heart cleansing. Amen.

Why I Believe in Holiness

William S. Deal

I wish to present here the reasons why I believe in holiness of heart and life. By holiness I mean that experience of God's grace where the heart is cleansed from all sin, and the believer is filled with the Holy Spirit in His abiding fullness.

John Wesley, Methodism's famous founder, variously referred to this experience as "Christian perfection," "entire sanctification," being "made perfect in love," and "the second blessing, properly so called."

Joseph H. Smith, for 60 years a Methodist evangelist and proponent and defender of the experience of sanctification, explained the meaning of Christian perfection in these words: "A *perfect separation* from one's self and presentation to Christ. A *perfect purification* of the heart from the blight and being of indwelling sin. A *perfect union* with God through the inhabitation of the Holy Spirit." *(Pauline Perfection,* p. 130.)

Here are the five reasons why I believe in holiness:

Because it is the moral nature of God

Of all the attributes of God, holiness is the most expressive of His moral perfection and character. It is the eternal counterbalance in the character of God. Without this distinct nature of His character there would be a deficiency in His being. If God were all-powerful but not holy, He would be a dangerous being, ungoverned by any counterbalancing influence. If God were all gracious and kind, but without holiness, He could become lenient and His universe would suffer moral decay. But as it is, His holiness balances all His other perfections — moral, ethical, and natural.

Since God has assigned to us in His Word the ideal of being like Him, it should be our highest aim to become like Him in personal character. Indeed, He said to Moses that the children of Israel were to have as their motto: "Ye shall be holy: for I the Lord your God am holy" (Leviticus 19:2).

Among the last words of Christ in His revelation to John was the final statement on holiness: "He that is holy, let him be holy still" (Revelation 22:11).

God's highest design for His people is that we may be "holy and without blame before Him in love" (Ephesians 1:4).

The only way this state can be attained is through Christ's sanctifying power in the heart, purifying the heart and bringing holiness of heart and godliness of life. Since it is God's perfect design for me to be holy, as He is, it is my greatest desire to fulfill that design.

It is the highest expression of God's will

Paul's explanation to the Thessalonians was in keeping with this highest expression of the will of God for us. "For this is the will of God, even your sanctification . . ." (I Thessalonians 4:3). While this sanctification doubtless refers to initial sanctification, which every believer experiences in regeneration, as he "starts on his way toward becoming fully sanctified," it does express the highest form of God's will for His children. Paul follows this up in verses 7 and 8 when he emphasizes that God has "called us unto holiness." He climaxes this teaching with his final prayer for the Thessalonians, "And the very God of peace sanctify you wholly; and I pray God your whole spirit and soul and body be preserved blameless unto the coming of our Lord Jesus Christ" (I Thessalonians 5:23). The word "wholly" here is better rendered "through and through," as the New International Version has it.

The will of God is the highest expression of the character and purpose of God. As such it is His chief desire and plan for His children.

Since I can seek no higher nor nobler aim or experience than the will of God in my life, therefore I believe that it is my duty to seek and find this experience of sanctification as soon as I know about it.

Holiness was made available to me in atonement

Whatever God has willed for His children, He has made available to them in practical life. For God to demand something of His people He did not provide and make available to them would be preposterous. It would be contrary to the nature of God and to His goodness, mercy, and love, as well as to His intelligent government of His children.

The whole scheme of redemption centers around this one essential purpose — to make man holy through Christ. The Hebrew writer proclaims this truth beautifully: "Wherefore Jesus, also, that He might sanctify the people with His own blood, suffered without the gate . . ." (Hebrews 13:12). Jesus asked the Father in His prayer, "Sanctify them through thy truth: thy word is truth . . . For their sakes I sanctify myself, that they also might be sanctified" (John 17:17, 19). Here the two meanings of the word *sanctify* come out forcibly. In verse 17 He is praying that they may be purified, purged, cleansed, made holy, while in verse 19, He is telling the Father that He now dedicates, consecrates, gives himself wholly to the cross of redemption that they may be sanctified in the sense of verse 17. Christ had no sin; therefore, He could not purge, cleanse, or purify himself; but He could dedicate and consecrate himself to the task of human redemption by His death on the cross.

Since by His death for me He provided for my sanctification, I am under solemn obligation either to seek, find, live, and enjoy this experience, or reject His atonement for it.

It is God's requirement of all men to be made holy

Starting with Leviticus 19:2, "Ye shall be holy: for I the Lord your God am holy," and going through the Scriptures to Revelation 22:11, "He that is holy, let him be holy still," there is no rest from the cry of prophet, priest, preacher, apostle, and disciple who spoke or wrote on the subject. They were all beseeching, commanding, exhorting, and persuading men to seek to be made holy. This call to be holy thunders in the law, shouts in the prophecies, sings in the psalms, whispers in the promises, supplicates in the prayers, urges in the commands, and rejoices in the testimonies of all Bible literature. It rises in the poetic fountain of Genesis 1:1 and culminates in the all-glorious River of Life in Revelation 22:1-2. It cries in the dying voice of every sacrificial animal, leaps up in the flames of every fiery altar, ascends heavenward in the smoke of every sacrifice of the Old Testament. It is in some way foreshadowed in all the old Levitical system, comes through in every Old Testament allegory, shines out of the life stories of all the worthies of faith, until it climaxes in a grand crescendo at the birth of the Babe of Bethlehem. It is in the background and framework of every parable, shows through as the ultimate purpose of every healing, and it is the dynamic behind all the Saviour's teachings. There is no higher line of thought and no greater purpose in view in all redemption's ministries than that man should ultimately be made holy.

"Blessed are the pure in heart, for they shall see God" (Matthew 5:8) is the positive way of saying, "Follow peace with all men, and holiness, without which no man shall see the Lord" (Hebrews 12:14).

Many professing Christians who refuse to seek heart holiness vainly imagine that God will in some way "get them by" without this holiness. He won't. One can not willingly, knowingly, and intentionally reject God's sanctifying grace and continue to be ready for heaven. Every truly saved person who "walks in the light as He is in the light" (I John 1:7), will either be *experientially* or *meritoriously* sanctified, whether he understands it or not. And every saved person who sees the light of holiness and refuses to walk in it will finally backslide because of his rebellion and rejection. He must either repent of his rejection, accept the "truth" as it is in Christ Jesus," and be sanctified, or finally become lost forever!

It meets man's moral and spiritual need

In both the Old and New Testaments multitudes of people have witnessed to the joy of a pure heart and a met need. There were two crises in the life of Abraham: First, when he said good-bye to Ur of the Chaldees and started to follow God, being "justified by faith" (Genesis 12). Second, when he heard the voice of God saying, "I am the Almighty God; walk before me, and be thou perfect" (Genesis 17:1). The outstanding change comes out in God's extending of the covenant and greatly increasing it, and in changing his name from Abram to Abraham. (See Genesis 17:2-8.)

Isaiah's cleansed life shines out in his gladsome response to God's call (Isaiah 6:5-8). It is especially seen in the cleansed lips, signifying a cleansed heart.

The New Testament is replete with instances of people receiving the Spirit's baptism and sanctifying grace after conversion (Acts 2:2-4; 8:14-17; 10:44-47; 11:1-18; 19:1-6).

All one needs to do is to look up the many references to cleansing, sanctification, holiness, and the Spirit's baptism in the New Testament to see that this was the crowning doctrine and experience of the apostles.

Millions throughout the ages since Pentecost have testified to the complete satisfaction in life and heart which this experience has brought to them. If experience and testimony are any part of the evidence, then this truth has been sealed by innumerable witnesses in all ages, and by all types of persons — rich and poor, educated and ignorant, healthy and sickly, all over the world.

The Holy Spirit's infilling in my teenage life and His constantly abiding presence with me has meant more to me than everything else in all my life. If you are not now enjoying this sanctifying fullness, let me urge you to now seek and find it.

Paul's Plea For Purity

Herbert Dongell

Paul's letters are dominated by pleas which he directs toward new Christians. In the Galatian letter he pleads the necessity of guarding spiritual freedom and not falling again into the bondage of legalism. The letter to the Romans is a plea for justification by faith in contrast to the notion of justification by works. When writing to the Corinthians, Paul pleads for unity among the brotherhood; he also declared that schisms over spiritual gifts or abilities should not be allowed. Other examples of strong exhortations could be cited, such as his pleas about being prepared for the Lord's return.

In chapters 3-5 of his first letter to the Thessalonians, Paul proclaims his plea for heart purity. This doctrine is clearly taught, not as a religious luxury, but rather as a spiritual necessity. To Paul, holiness of heart was basic to a viable Christian experience. His purged heart made it possible for him to be faithful to God under the most trying conditions. The apostle was convinced that God's purpose for all His children is "To the end He may stablish your heart unblamable in holiness before God, even our Father, at the coming of our Lord Jesus Christ with all His saints" (I Thessalonians 3:13). In I Thessalonians 4:2 the apostle declares holiness to be a *commandment of the Lord Jesus.* By these words we understand that this experience is not optional. No doubt Paul had in mind the counsel and commandment of God to Moses (Leviticus 11:44): "For I am the Lord your God: ye shall therefore sanctify yourselves, and ye shall be holy; for I am holy. . . ." Peter continues this thought in respect to its fulfillment: "Be ye holy, for I am holy" (I Peter 3:16). Paul, along with Peter, is inspired to reveal that the Heavenly Father knows what is best for His children and acts accordingly.

The command that His children be like the Father demonstrates the highest degree of divine affection. This is no straitjacket compulsion or bondage, but rather an invitation to the highest calling of God, who originated the plan and rejoices in its effectiveness in the lives of His children who claim His purifying power.

The apostle continues in I Thessalonians 4:3 by declaring that this establishing grace is the *will of God*. The word "will" indicates this experience to be God's volitional choice and the supreme desire for each of His children. The revealed purpose in this injunction is for moral purity — "to abstain from fornication." However we interpret and translate the word for "vessel" (as "wife" or as "body"), the end result is the same. God expects and demands His people to be free from physical and mental immorality.

Obviously, then, this condition of purity must be attained in the heart. "As a man thinketh in his heart, so is he" (Proverbs 23:7). "Blessed are the pure in heart for they shall see God" (Matthew 5:8). In a world of wanton lust and "free love," a person can become holy and remain pure only as he, by faith, claims God's abundant cleansing and keeping grace. Thus he is able to escape the designs of Satan and, consequently, avoid the wrath of God.

In I Thessalonians 4:7 the apostle further declares that holiness is God's *call to the thirsty, longing heart*. To be called to partake of God's holiness is the greatest of all honors, and it is the highest of all divine invitations because it is a call to share God's own nature. Holiness is more than a gift or an experience; it is a union with divinity — becoming a partaker of the divine nature (II Peter 1:4).

The importance of the call is stressed by a warning, namely, that whoever rejects this call shows disrespect for God, who has given to us His Holy Spirit. The value that the Lord places on this heavenly calling cannot be overestimated. It deserves our honest, sincere, and prayerful consideration.

Holiness of heart is the *work of God.* From I Thessalonians 5:23, "And may the God of peace himself sanctify you to be whole ones" (literal translation), we understand that God is the One who sanctifies the human heart and spirit. It is not an accomplishment of man through good works or strong desires. Rather, it is a divine operation of the Holy Spirit who, in a moment, completes the purifying of the believing heart and makes it spiritually whole. Just as God instantly forgives the penitent and contrite sinner, so God cleanses carnality or inbred sin from the heart of His seeking child (I John 1:9).

Paul assures his readers that this consecrated relationship with God secures the preservation of spirit, soul, and body until the coming of the Lord.

Can such an experience of heart purity be obtained now? Is this more than we can expect or hope? Listen to God's answer through Paul's Spirit-inspired pen: "Faithful is he that calleth you who also will do it" (I Thessalonians 5:24). The faithfulness of God is the answer to all our perplexities about obtaining a pure heart. He is faithful to spare our physical lives according to His providential will (v. 23); He is faithful to convict of sin (John 16:8); He is faithful to regenerate (I John 1:9); He is faithful to cleanse our souls (I Thessalonians 5:23-24); He is faithful to deliver us from temptation (I Corinthians 10:13); and He will be faithful to present us faultless before the presence of

His glory with exceeding joy (Jude 24).

   Paul's plea for purity is ultimately *God's plea*. Purity is God's command, God's will, God's call, God's work, and the objective of God's faithfulness! Let us then believe these promises, claim His cleansing power, and prove His faithfulness! Then by His grace we shall be ready to live, to serve, to die, or to meet Him at His soon return.

The Central Idea of Christianity

L. B. Reese

Bishop Jessie T. Peck uses the caption *The Central Idea of Christianity* as the title of his book on holiness.

In one of the opening statements, Peck says: "The interpretation of a system depends upon its central idea. This is seen in mechanism. The different parts of a watch, for instance, would be perfectly unintelligible to the most careful observer without the idea which produced it."

We can discern the central idea of Christianity when we closely study Ephesians 1:4 and interpret it in context. Paul here states, "According as he hath chosen us in him before the foundation of the world, that we should be holy and without blame before him in love."

In Ephesians 1:4, we have:
   (1) The purpose declared,
   (2) The people designated, and
   (3) The perimeter delineated.

The word *according* is a key word in Ephesians chapters 1—3. In three chapters, Paul uses this word twelve times. One exegete notes the following: "They either point out how the great blessings of Christ's mission have underlying them the divine *purpose,* or they point out how the process of the Christian life in the individual has for its source and *measure* the abundances, the wealth of the grace and the power of God."

We may conclude that the word "according" in Ephesians 1:4 belongs in the first class: that of declaring the purpose of God. This purpose is spelled out in such statements as "according to the good pleasure of his will," "according to his good pleasure which he purposed in himself," and "according to the purpose of him who worketh all things after the counsel of his own will."

The sovereign will of God displayed by this passage points up the content and dynamic of God's purpose. Men have always been inspired by a sense of the sovereign will of God motivating their actions.

The people to whom the words of this text are addressed are those whom Paul calls the "new man"; those who are fully described in Ephesians 2:13-22. These are the Jews and Gentiles to whom the mystery of redemption has been revealed.

The perimeter of God's purpose is clarified by the thoughts suggested by the term "holy," which is the positive aspect; "without blame" is the negative, and "before him in love" reveals the place and motive which fulfills the whole purpose of God.

In view of this perimeter of the divine purpose: holiness, the word of separation, implies we are to be different from the common run of men. William Barclay puts it succinctly when he states: "Holy is the Greek word *'hagios,'* which always has in it the idea of difference and separation . . . So, then, God chose the Christian that he should be different from other men."

Both Adam Clarke and Barclay call attention to the fact that "blameless" is a sacrificial term. The sacrifices were to be free from all blemishes. In summing up, Barclay makes the pertinent remark: "This word does not mean the Christian must be respectable; it means that he must be perfect."

The whole thrust of the text is both modified and intensified by the appeal "before him in love." This on the one hand relieves us from the exactions of men, but insists on the requirements of God as seen in the light of continual "God-awareness."

God has had only one plan from the foundation of the world. The fall of man necessitated no afterthought. God has always had the same objective expressed in the phrases "blessed us," "chosen us," "predestinated us," and "made us." This is the totality of His redemption in Jesus — provisioned in the past, executed in the present, and finalized in the future.

All time and eternity will be needed for us to fully comprehend all that is involved in His plan — a plan expressed in the words of Ephesians 1:4 — "According as he hath chosen us in him before the foundation of the world, that we should be holy and without blame before him in love."

That Missing Note of Victory

Harold K. Sheets

Few who read these lines would question that the sanctified life is a New Testament privilege for Christians. In varying degrees of clarity this truth has been presented to us. The doctrine of sanctifying grace has been a part of our heritage.

What is more, the crisis and the process are two well-recognized aspects of the sanctified life. Many, however, will recall when the crisis aspects were emphasized to the neglect of progressive aspects of this walk with the Lord. How the church suffers from those who try to get enough grace for a lifetime out of the initial crisis experience!

Now the tables seem to be turning. Whatever point is made of Christian growth and maturity, the place of the crisis as the gateway into the sanctified life is being obscured or neglected. In the judgment of this writer, the neglect is a very serious one. Both aspects are essential and biblical.

For, when the crisis is lost, the distinctness of sanctifying grace is lost. Moreover, the occasion for the song of rejoicing is lacking. It is perhaps life's greatest victory when the powerful forces of evil arrayed against holiness in the heart are defeated, attitudes are made right, and perfect love has its beginning. Praise becomes spontaneous. Otherwise the Christian life must be pursued below the level of this finished epochal grace with all the attendant pitfalls, perils, and defeats of such a life. Here, as in war among nations, "There is no substitute for victory."

Both in the Old and New Testaments the exercise of faith is supremely commended. And the Scriptures make faith an essential element in pressing into the sanctified life. The crisis gateway into this life is, I believe, entirely compatible with this faith.

Think of the many crisis victories in Bible history: the Red Sea and Jordan crossings; the tumbling walls at Jericho; Sarah's conception of Isaac; Elijah's chariot of fire; the descending dove upon our Lord in Jordan; Peter's deliverance from prison; and others. One could not fit these events into anything less than a crisis situation. Using the crisis of entire sanctification as a parallel, I believe, is not a forced but a natural application of the exercise of faith.

This epochal victory, moreover, lays the foundation for rejoicing and celebration. Nobody builds a bonfire, calls out the band, waves the banners, and fills the air with jubilee until there is a victory. And when there is a victory, whether on the battlefield or on the athletic field, who can restrain the celebration? We do not celebrate our victory with the world's hilarity, but with the song of the conqueror — the worship experience which finds release in joyful, sometimes spontaneous expression.

There is also that witness to others of the reality of the cleansing fountain. The challenge to the preacher or teacher is to consistently urge believers to press their way by faith, so that, whether at church altars or informal wrestling places with God, souls find no rest until they find that sanctifying rest from inward defeat.

It is possible to preach about sanctification in such a way that it does not dawn upon the listener to definitely seek the experience. It is also possible, however, to both live and preach the entirely sanctified life in such a way that people are made hungry, and understand the steps of obedience and faith by which they may obtain this blessed victory.

A boy was tediously at work with his piano lesson. His father, sensitive to music, was listening from another room. The boy labored through seven notes of the octave, then left the piano, omitting the eighth note. The father, anticipating the eighth note, and torn by the incompleteness, rushed to the piano and sounded the note to complete the octave.

Holiness is the note needed in Christian testimony today — the note of victory, and completeness. God, sensitive to the triumph of His atonement, is listening for that note. It is the note that makes His will complete. It is the hallelujah note in every tongue on earth and in the songs of heaven.

Will you allow Him to make complete His work in you?

Experiential Sanctification

W. L. Surbrook

"Sanctify them through thy truth: thy word is truth" (John 17:17). That statement is lifted out of the heart of Jesus' high-priestly prayer in which He was praying for the sanctification of His faithful followers. His prayer indicates that the deep burden of His heart was for their sanctification.

It was for the purpose of bringing His followers into the experience of heart cleansing that the resurrected Jesus "commanded them that they should not depart from Jerusalem, but wait for the promise of the Father" (Acts 1:4). The promise of the Father was fulfilled on the day of Pentecost when the believers "were all filled with the Holy Ghost" (Acts 2:4).

Entire sanctification is a second definite, instantaneous work of grace wrought in the heart following regeneration. The new birth (initial sanctification) is a powerful and glorious work of grace which deals primarily with the forgiveness of our sins and a change in the direction of our lives, but it does not remove the basic selfishness and rebellion of the heart which theologians call the carnal nature.

After one is converted and continues to prayerfully walk in the light, he will discover he still has an internal enemy, the carnal nature, which tends to rebel against what he knows to be right. In this condition the Scriptures picture him as a "double-minded man [who] is unstable in all his ways" (James 1:8). He has the mind of Christ, but he still has the carnal mind. If he will pray, humble his heart, dedicate his life entirely to God and by faith trust Him, the Holy Spirit will entirely cleanse this carnal nature out of his heart and he will enjoy the fullness of the Holy Spirit. In this act the Holy Spirit completely cleanses his heart of all sin, and entire sanctification becomes his glorious experience.

The importance of the clear teaching of both conversion and entire sanctification has characterized the holiness movement from its inception.

In his sermon entitled "Sin in Believers," John Wesley goes on record with clarity:

> "By sin I here understand inward sin; any sinful temper, passion, or affection; such as pride, self-will, love of the world, in any kind or degree; such as lust, anger, peevishness; any disposition contrary to the mind of Christ. . . . Is a justified or regenerated man freed from all sin as soon as he is justified? . . . Was he not then freed from all sin, so that there is no sin in his heart? I cannot say this; I cannot believe it; because St. Paul says to the contrary. He is speaking to believers in general when he says, The flesh lusteth against the Spirit, and the Spirit against the flesh: and these are contrary the one to the other. Gal. 5:17. Nothing could be more expressive. The apostle here directly affirms that the flesh, evil Nature, opposes the Spirit, even in believers; that even in the regenerate there are two principles, contrary the one to the other."

I appreciate the quotation on this subject from *Introduction to Christian Theology*, (p. 314) by the late H. Orton Wiley, S.T.D.

> *"A Definition of Entire Sanctification"*
> "We believe that entire sanctification is that act of God, subsequent to regeneration, by which believers are made free from original sin or depravity, and brought into a state of full devotement to God, and holy obedience of love made perfect. It is wrought by the baptism with the Holy

Spirit, and comprehends in one experience the cleansing of the heart from sin, and the abiding, indwelling presence of the Holy Spirit empowering the believer for life and service. Entire sanctification is provided by the blood of Jesus; is wrought instantaneously by faith; preceded by entire consecration; and to this work and state of grace the Holy Spirit bears witness."

Perhaps a greater understanding of these two works of grace can be gained by contrasting them as follows:

1. Regeneration is a new birth; sanctification is a death to the carnal nature.
2. Regeneration is an impartation of a new life; sanctification is an expurgation or cleansing out of an old life.
3. Regeneration gives one something he has never had; sanctification delivers him from something he has always had.
4. Regeneration gives a person the new man; sanctification delivers him from the old man.
5. Regeneration gives love; sanctification gives perfect love.
6. Regeneration pardons the acts of sin; sanctification purges out the principle of sin.
7. Regeneration gives life; sanctification gives the more abundant life.
8. Regeneration removes the guilt of sin; sanctification destroys the internal power of sin.
9. Regeneration makes possible our adoption into God's family; sanctification restores the moral image of God to the soul.
10. Regeneration gives one a title to heaven; sanctification gives him fitness for heaven.
11. At the instant that one is regenerated, he is also justified and adopted; at the instant of sanctification his heart is cleansed from the principle of original sin and filled with the Holy Spirit.

In conclusion, let me again quote from *Introduction to Christian Theology.*

"The extent of cleansing, according to the Scriptures, includes the complete removal of all sin. Sin is to be cleansed thoroughly, purged, extirpated, eradicated, and crucified; not repressed, suppressed, counteracted, or made void as these terms are commonly used. It is to be destroyed; and any theory which makes a place for the existence of inbred sin, whatever the provisions made for its regulation, is unscriptural."

Endowment of Power

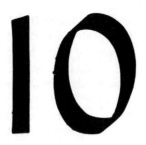

J. A. Coffey

Jesus told His disciples, "Ye shall receive power, after that the Holy Ghost is come upon you: and ye shall be witnesses unto me . . ." (Acts 1:8). To study the lives of those men is to discover their need for power. Their fellowship had been haunted continually by motives which revealed jealousy, selfishness, division, envy, and strife; many of these they would later call carnal. Their hearts must have often been convicted as they heard Jesus' message, knowing that their lives were so often a contradiction to His teaching.

If the life and teachings of Christ were going to be perpetuated on this earth, then the coming of the Holy Spirit must be with such an endowment of power that it would reach to the very basis of their lives. Pentecost proved to be just that, in its purifying and empowering aspects.

Scripturally the word *purity* means, "singleness of heart," a heart that is no longer divided. "Cleanse your hands ye sinners and purify your hearts ye double-minded" (James 4:8). Second, it means to be without defilement or cleansed. The Word says, "Christ gave himself for us, that he might redeem us from all iniquity, and purify unto himself a peculiar people zealous of good works" (Titus 2:14).

In connection with the gospel call to the Gentiles, the strong defense of Peter was the direct correlation between the baptism of the Holy Spirit and the purifying of the believer's heart. He said to the Council, "And God which knoweth the hearts bare them witness, giving them the Holy Spirit, even as he did unto us, and put no difference between us and them, purifying their hearts by faith" (Acts 15:8-9). Some authors feel that possibly fifteen years may have passed since Pentecost. After those years, what remained significant to Peter, was not the noise of a rushing mighty wind or the cloven tongues of fire, or the gift of other languages. It was the *purifying of the heart* in response to faith and the fullness of the Holy Spirit.

The gospel of Christ is concerned with the *heart,* the center of man's being and personality, the fount out of which comes everything else. Thus, the Christian life is ultimately not a matter of doctrine or understanding; it is a condition of the heart. In relation to the filling of the Holy Spirit, that condition is purity. Purity is power, for as the soul is cleansed it is filled and empowered by the Spirit.

What a change Pentecost wrought in those disciples' lives. Samuel Chadwick has stated so eloquently, "Fear had gone, they no longer sat with closed windows and bolted doors for fear of the Jews. They feared no one. They were afraid of nothing. They no longer spoke with bated breath. They proclaimed the truth concerning Jesus in the open streets of the city where Jesus had been murdered — and that within six weeks of his death. A new power was at work. The world had never seen such a day. The angels had never seen such a day. Neither had Satan and his hosts of spiritual darkness ever seen such a day. The vital thing that happened at Pentecost is that the Spirit of Jesus came to abide in the hearts of men in the power of God."

The acts done by the apostles are the credentials of

their effective witness to the power of the Holy Spirit's invasion, which so possessed their lives with dynamic power and authority that in a few years they had "turned their world upside down" (Acts 17:6).

I believe that God's recipe is still the same for reaching today's world. Could it be that while we have been spending inordinate amounts of time and energy to discover innovations to stimulate and motivate our Church, that God is simply seeking ordinary people the Holy Spirit can cleanse and fill for His glory? God wants to fill ordinary people with extraordinary power. He desires to turn baffled faith into a rapturous conquest. And that is what holiness is all about.

The Basic Truth of Pentecost

Robert H. Heckart

The Apostle Peter gives what I consider to be the basic truth of Pentecost in his climactic statement to the Jerusalem Church Council. He said, "And God which knoweth the hearts, bare them witness, giving them [the Gentiles] the Holy Ghost, even as he did unto us; [the Jews] and put no difference between us and them, purifying their hearts by faith" (Acts 15:8-9).

Pentecost was a Jewish feast day. It became a historical Christian event when the descent of the Holy Spirit and the beginning of the Christian church occurred on that day. It is significant to us because it is also a present-day religious experience (Acts 2:37-39).

Yes, the promise is to *us*, to our children, and to all afar off, both chronologically and geographically. This is the phase of Pentecost I wish to discuss.

On the initial Christian Pentecost there were outward manifestations: a rushing mighty wind, cloven tongues of fire, and the speaking in tongues. Many persons, both then and now, experience the Christian Pentecost without sensing any special movement of the wind, or without receiving the ability of speaking in another language. The Bible records five great church Pentecosts (Acts 2, 4, 8, 10, 19). In four of these instances nothing is said about a rushing wind or tongues of fire. In two (Acts

4, 8) nothing is said concerning speaking in tongues. So, none of these three outward manifestations can be considered as the basic truth of Pentecost.

Beyond these outward manifestations there were inward and personal experiences. These four inward experiences relate to the basic truth of Pentecost as I see it.

First, they received the promise of the Father (Luke 24:49; Acts 1:4; John 16:7, 13). This is not a reference to one of the thousands of promises recorded in God's Word, but is a direct reference to a specific promise by God concerning the incoming, the infilling and the indwelling of the Holy Spirit.

Second, they were baptized with the Holy Spirit (Acts 1:5). There are many infillings and anointings, but only one baptism with the Spirit. Jesus was filled and anointed with the Spirit (Luke 4:1, 18). He was never baptized with the Spirit. The baptism with the Spirit has to do with the sin problem — inbred sin or the carnal nature. Since Jesus was not born in sin, He did not need the baptism with the Spirit. You and I do.

Third, they were cleansed from sin. In that Jerusalem council meeting Peter did not say, "Those Gentiles heard the sound of a rushing mighty wind just like we did." Nor did he say, "Cornelius and his group saw and felt cloven tongues of fire resting upon them even as we did." Neither did he say, "Those Roman or Gentile believers all spoke with other tongues just like we all did." What did he say? He told them that God gave them the Holy Ghost "and put no difference between us and them, *purifying their hearts by faith.*" This then is the basic truth of Pentecost. Purity. Purity is what we must preach and experience. Purity is what we must insist our hearers and seekers receive. The outward manifestations — rushing winds, cloven tongues, and other languages — are outward symbols, ecstasies, and embellishments of the essential indispensable cleansing of the heart. Purity is God's requirement for our entrance into the celestial city. The Greek rendering of Hebrews 12:14 is: "Follow peace with all men and the sanctification without which no man shall see the Lord."

Fourth, they were endued with the Holy Spirit's power (Greek: Dynamite!) (Luke 24:49; Acts 1:8). This is not power to do the spectacular. But it is power which changed a cowardly vacillating Peter into a bulwark of spiritual fortitude and transformed a "son of thunder" John into an apostle of love. It is that power which enables one to become a child of God (John 1:12); to keep saved (I Peter 1:5); to be sanctified wholly (I Thessalonians 5:23); have power over one's own will (I Corinthians 7:37); to preach (I Corinthians 2:4); to witness (Acts 1:8, 4:33); to overcome obstacles (Zechariah 4:6); to walk with God (Isaiah 40:31).

It is thrilling to "fly"; it is joyous to "run"; but it is the daily grind of life — "the walk" — which saps our strength. Thank God, this power enables us to "walk and not faint!"

The basic truth of Pentecost relates to the *inward* experiences of the event. We should emphasize the promise of the Father, the baptism of the Holy Spirit, the cleansing from sin, and the resulting power for a fruitful life of service.

May God help us preach, testify, and live this heart-cleansing, life-transforming doctrine and experience of second-blessing holiness.

Steps to the Spirit-Filled Life 12

Joe C. Sawyer

How can one be sanctified — filled with the Holy Spirit?

One purpose of the Holy Spirit is to bring the born-again Christian into the fully sanctified life, an experience of the cleansing, filling, and indwelling of the Spirit. Holiness is a state, the result of being entirely sanctified; entire sanctification is the act of cleansing. This experience is for the believer who is enjoying saving grace. Receiving the Holy Spirit's cleansing and power in our lives is a simple process; however, we must follow the New Testament pattern. Six steps can bring the believer into this experience of receiving the Spirit in all His fullness and power.

Step One — Realization

Realize your need for cleansing

The first step is to realize your need for cleansing. There must first be an awareness of the need for cleansing and being filled with the Spirit. Man is sinful by nature. Six exists in a twofold sense. First, there are the actual sinful deeds which are committed. Separation from God and guilt are incurred as a result of this sinful action. Forgiveness and regeneration through faith in Christ constitute the new birth — a saving relationship with Christ.

In the second place, sin is a state of inward corruption and defilement which requires cleansing. The command by Paul in Ephesians 5:18 and David's prayer in Psalm 51:10 bring our need into focus. This realization of our need must become a conviction, thrusting us on our way toward the remedy.

Step Two — Desire

Desire the filling of the Spirit

The second step is desire. The believer must earnestly *desire* the cleansing and filling of the Holy Spirit. The sense of need leads to this strong desire, firm resolution, and earnest seeking for this grace provided and promised by the Lord Jesus himself (Matthew 5:6; Acts 1:8). A consuming desire for the fullness of the Holy Spirit's blessing to be revealed in our lives should possess us. Proper cultivation of this desire hastens our approach to step three.

Step Three — Confession

Confess your need and obey God's Word

Step three centers around confession. Confess your need and obey God's Word. The Christian must see his need of cleansing, admit it, sincerely confess the need to God, willingly obey the Lord, and walk in the light (I John 1:7-9). There is no substitute for obedience (Acts 5:32). God's willingness to bestow something always matches our preparedness to receive it. Our obedience now becomes our confession of need for the fullness of the Holy Spirit. This should result in a willing confession that promises to commit our all to God.

Step Four — Consecration

Consecrate yourself, body, mind, soul to God

Consecration constitutes step four. Consecrate yourself, mind, body, and soul to God. Consecration is your part of the contract. It is an act of the will, a deliberate choice to give your heart, your will, your abilities, your talents — your all — to God. Paul in Romans 12:1 said, "Present your bodies a living sacrifice, holy, acceptable unto God, which is your reasonable service." God will not fill what He does not have; therefore, surrender and submission to Him are vital. What God receives He cleanses, fills, and sanctifies for His use and service. The Christian consecrates, but the Holy Spirit cleanses and fills. The faithfulness of God in fulfilling His promise is seen in I Thessalonians 5:23. Make this a very meaningful and decisive act as you totally surrender to the Lord. This is a voluntary and unconditional surrender of self, motives, and purpose to God's will for you. It is here that a crisis takes place; self is crucified and Christ begins to reign supreme. Spirit-filled living begins with a total commitment to God without reservations (Romans 6:4-6). Remember, Christ will never do more *through* you than He is permitted to do *in* you. Therefore, through a definite act of consecration give yourself wholly to God (I Thessalonians 5:23). After you have done this, you can experience step five.

Step Five — Cleansing

Ask God for the cleansing and filling of the Spirit

Step five deals with cleansing. Here we ask God for the cleansing and filling of the Holy Spirit. Remember, we consecrate, but *the Lord* cleanses and prepares the heart where He desires to dwell in His fullness. This crisis of cleansing and filling becomes a beginning for a life of fullness and greater conquest. Having confessed our condition, failures, lacks, and sinful nature, cleansing through the blood of Christ becomes a reality. "Create in me a clean heart, O God" was David's prayer (Psalm 51:7, 10).

> So wash me, Thou, without, within;
> Or purge with fire, if that must be.
> No matter how, if only sin
> Die out in me, die out in me.
>
> Walter C. Smith

We can count on the faithfulness of God to do His office work in our hearts. Paul said, "Faithful is He that calleth you who also will do it" (I Thessalonians 5:24). We must ask God to cleanse and fill us with His Holy Spirit. In Luke 11:9 and 13, Jesus said, "Ask, and it shall be given you; seek, and ye shall find; knock, and it shall be opened unto you. . . . If ye . . . know how to give good gifts unto your children; how much more shall your heavenly father give the Holy Spirit to them that ask him?"

We are at the point now where we must take one additional step in order to fully enter into the reality of the Spirit-filled life.

Step Six — Claiming

Exercise faith for cleansing and filling of the Spirit

Step six is claiming the experience through faith. We exercise faith and believe God to sanctify us and fill us with His Holy Spirit. There is a definite moment of entering into this state of grace. The key word is faith, an act of appropriating His word. God wants His children to know the rich measure of the Spirit's possession and leadership. All that remains is for us to claim this experience.

The Bible speaks clearly at this point, for we read in Acts 15:8-9, "God, who knoweth the hearts, bare them witness, giving them the Holy Ghost, even as He did unto us; and put no difference between us and them, purifying their hearts by faith." Paul in Galatians 3:2-4 asks, ". . . received ye the Spirit by the works of the law, or by the hearing of faith?" Peter said, "Seeing ye have purified your souls in obeying the truth through the Spirit . . ." (I Peter 1:22). We have seen the need, we have consecrated our all, we have made the surrender complete, and now we commit and believe the Holy Spirit to cleanse and to come into His temple. We believe God.

The Holy Spirit is always faithful to impart assurance, evidence, and witness to the heart that the work has been accomplished. The definite crisis experience of sanctification must not be confused with the times of repeated renewal and anointing by the Spirit in the life of the believer. Replenishments are part of the Spirit's enablements. Basically entire sanctification is a baptism of love. It is the beginning of Spirit-filled living.

The testimony of Samuel Chadwick can be of help to us, as it has helped others in the past. He said,

> When I was twenty-three, I had been preaching about seven years, and had fifteen sermons. I thought those fifteen sermons would turn the world upside down. When I had preached them, there were not fifteen more people in the chapel than when I started. When I was confronted with this proposition in May 1882, God enlightened my conscience and opened my eyes to the need of some reinforcements of power. When I became filled with the Holy Spirit, every part of my being awakened. I did not get a new set of brains, but I got a new mentality. I did not get a new faculty of speech, but I got a new effectiveness of speech. I did not get a new dictionary, but a new Bible. Immediately I was a new creature, with the same basis of natural qualities that were energized, vitalized, reinforced and quickened into a bigger vitality and effectiveness that nobody would ever have dreamed possible. That is what happens to everybody upon whom the Spirit comes.

I was converted as a teen at the altar in Salem Methodist Church, Independence, Virginia. Conversion was real, resulting in a transformation of life, conduct, and Christian witness. Later on, at times, my life became an up-and-down experience, clouded with traits of carnality or manifestations that were short of total victory. Inwardly, I felt God had something more — a total remedy. My awakening to the need of heart holiness came rather suddenly after hearing the truth preached. I was led into the experience some months later at the Gordon Camp Meeting in Gordon, Nebraska, under the ministry of O. G. Wilson. I prayed a simple prayer and received this blessing.

I had done all that was required, and in faith and obedience I was claiming all that God had for me. The witness of the Spirit fully came to my heart late that same night as I told a dear friend of my newfound victory in Christ. As I shared, the love, presence, and warmth of God's love engulfed my whole being. It felt like a warm glow was moving through my entire being. Joy flooded my soul. It dawned on me that this was the witness of the Holy Spirit that He had come to dwell in His fullness; He was now enthroned.

It is comforting and refreshing to still sense His warmth and wonderful presence within. The manifestation or witness may be different for you; nevertheless, the relationship and experience will be real.

Consider these thoughts as you allow God to deal with you —

What I give God takes (Romans 12:12);
What He takes, He cleanses (I John 1:7-9);
What He cleanses, He fills (Ephesians 5:18, 19);
What He fills, He seals (Ephesians 1:13); and
What He seals, He uses (II Timothy 2:21).

—A. Paget Wilkes